I Believe
in
Justice and Hope

I Believe
in
Justice and Hope

PEDRO CASALDALIGA, CMF

Notre Dame, Indiana 46556

Translated by Joseph C. Daries, CMF

Cover photo by Richard Todd, CMF

© COPYRIGHT, 1978: FIDES/CLARETIAN
NOTRE DAME, INDIANA

Library of Congress Cataloging in Publication Data

Casaldáliga, Pedro.
  I believe in justice and hope.

    Translation of Yo creo en la justicia y en la
esperanza!
    1. Casaldáliga, Pedro.   2.   Catholic Church—
Bishops—Biography. 3.   Bishops—Brazil—Biography.
4.   Church and social problems—Brazil. 5.   Church
and social problems—Catholic Church.   6.   Christianity
and justice. I. Title.
BX4705.C33547A3813   282′.092′4 [B]   78-21694
ISBN 0-8190-0628-9

Published originally by Desclée de Brouwer (Bilbao), copyright 1977.

11785

Contents

A Letter
To Pedro Casaldaliga

DEAR FRIEND PEDRO:
  You left it up to me to get someone to write a foreword
in your book. Frankly, your credo needs no foreword.
People already know about you and about your suffering people's church in São Félix. Any reader can discover
the real *you* in these pages without the help of an an-
nouncer or guide. You live your faith openheartedly and,
in confessing it, you hold nothing back. You have set aside
all inhibitions, and your words flame forth in the freest of
Christian freedoms.
  Many people will be startled to hear a bishop speaking
out the way you do. Some will be scandalized at the options
you have chosen, at your denunciations, at the fearless
critical realism of your faith. Others, on the contrary, will
label your ministry as too "sacral," and will regard your
options as naive and politically timid. Still others will be
upset and irritated at the way you dress!
  But no one will ever be able to deny that you are a man
who believes and who loves. Somewhere you say: "I state
all this so passionately, because this church, which I love so
very much, also pains me deeply." And the "life that has
given meaning to your credo"—the cruel, grinding life on
that Brazilian *sertão* of yours—has radicalized your faith
and turned it into something essential and hard, something that cannot be bought off. Of course, people who are

in the habit of watering down the scalding heat of faith and love with the tepid bath of their petty conveniences are going to find a faith and love without these painkillers to be a monstrous and insulting thing. The plain fact is, Pedro, that our world really can't stand love. It's gotten to the point where, even in the church, an out-and-out faith is as rare as it's dangerous.

For some churchfolk, your credo will be altogether too Christian.

But then you know that the one for whom your faith and hope are named—Jesus Christ—scandalized scribes, doctors, pharisees, and priests, disappointed those who wanted him to be a kind of political leader, and rubbed the whole religious and civil establishment of his day the wrong way. If he came back among us today, the same thing would happen all over again, even in our own church. Aren't many of the faithful being persecuted nowadays? And didn't he clearly tell us that this would be the case?

I think that your harshest criticisms and denunciations— the ones that a certain class of people will find most shocking—are really the "evidence" of a witness at a trial. Evidence that all of us, everywhere, repeat to one another in muffled tones. Common evidence!

But what is not at all common (even now, and most unfortunately), is to hear a bishop speak up and "tell it like it is." For the freedom with which you speak is no longer common in the church, as it once was in its earliest days. The vast majority of us Christians lack the freedom of a love born of faith. And since you are one of the "very few truly free persons" in our world, your voice compensates us somewhat for the silences of all too many religious superiors, bishops, archbishops, cardinals, and nuncios, and points an accusing finger at our own guilty silences. All of us should raise our voices in a fraternal outcry for the love of freedom—the freedom to which your "evidence" bears witness—so that your testimony may become common knowledge in the church: knowledge leading to conversion. This is the only kind of freedom that will make our faith consistent and convincing. And this kind of Christian freedom is something truly irreversible, since it is impelled by the Spirit of Truth.

Because this Spirit is alive and moving in our world, your credo will touch and free all those who recognize in it the voice of their own faith and love, of their agonies, of their hopes, and of their dreadful temptations to despair. Christians, men and women of conscience, communities, ordinary people, the simple, the poor, those who suffer the most—all these will hear your message. And these, Pedro, are the very seal of the Spirit of God.

And there are many of us half-converted Christians for whom your unbribable faith in justice and hope will be an awakening and a call to action.

Not a single article of your credo strikes me as odd or out of character. But as I have read it, I have come to a much clearer understanding of the radicalizing and purifying process your faith has undergone. The bits and pieces of your *Diary* which you have shared with us help us glimpse what has come to be the essence of your faith, your sorrow and your hope on that *sertão,* that forest, that river, and among those *sertanejo* Indians and peasants, all of them—land and people—chattels of a capitalism which is as voracious as it is unjust.

One thing I didn't know was that premature cataracts are causing you to lose your sight! Have you had them operated on yet? I know that it's a waste of time for me to tell you not to expose yourself to so many dangers, because even I can grasp (although not from personal experience) that, for someone whose whole life is an act of self-offering, to hold back anything would be a denial of his true self. But I will insist that anything you can do to get some rest and relaxation is a real duty for you, so that you can serve your beloved people better. So . . . take care!

In closing, I want to say that I hope this autobiography of your faith will not damage your literary reputation. On the contrary, I hope that all who read it will experience a surge of greater Christian freedom, leading to growth in a faith that is more truthful, realistic, and self-consistent.

I remain, your friend—and the friend of all your friends in the "Kingdom of Death and Hope"—where you cry out the silences of the people.

Teófilo Cabestrero, CMF

Introduction

After making the publisher wait patiently for a year and a half, I have finally given birth to this credo of mine. Believe me, the women of this *sertão* have a much easier time delivering their babies.

This child of mine had such a fidgety gestation that I'm afraid it's been born a bit feverish and windy, whimsical and poetic by turns, and somewhat bitter—but sincere. A lot like its father, I suppose.

José María de Llanos expressed a desire to be its godfather from the very beginning. "What people want," he told me, "is to hear what a bishop living among the outcasts of Brazil really believes in." He asked me to write a book that would be "all prayer and reminiscences," and one that would not be afraid of "doing a little disrobing in public; because," he added, "Christians are a bit fed up with books on spirituality, but not with books like this, that bear living witness. They want to know how and in what others believe—especially if those 'others' happen to be bishops."

It's true: we tend to believe along with others who believe. Faith is confession. And so I add this, my confession, to those of my predecessors.

As bishop of São Félix—especially after all the strange goings-on in my prelature—I had been thrust into the limelight (or rather, the pillory) of public attention. So it seemed to me that I might, or even, ought "to give an account of the hope that is in me."

Giving this account has somehow helped to ease the pain.

It has also been something of a response to the many friends who have so generously accompanied me along the way.

Perhaps it will have done a little to help someone believe in freedom, and to hunger and thirst after justice.

I've probably disappointed some and scandalized others. All I ask is to be read without preconceptions and with genuine freedom. After all, a bishop doesn't cease being a simple Christian man just because he's received the grace and the responsibility of serving his brothers and sisters fully.

My credo, as you will see, is doggedly clerical, because it's been clerical all my life. I have just one thing to ask of those friends who don't "have" the faith, of those who accept me for "other" reasons (at best and deep down, they are the same reasons), of those who never were or no longer are clerical: Please make the effort to distinguish between my clericalism (with all its little ironies), and my Christian faith.

The longest part of this book is dedicated to the "life that has given meaning to my credo." It deals with how I received the faith in my own particular life. How life has taught me to believe. How I planned to live what I believed in. How, by believing, I managed to live. How, by living, I came to believe more and better—or to just plain believe.

God takes hold of a person's life by making himself present to that person, and by giving him the grace to answer "Yes!" As Durrwell puts it: "The truly human way of giving something to God consists in accepting his gift." I am the first to admit that I have had what others have not had: an explicit encounter with God in Jesus Christ, in the midst of that community of faith which is his church. This is a mystery which has "bowled me over" and forced me to believe that God is bigger than all our hearts, our dogmas, and our communities.

Because I talk about *my* faith, I do so without blushing, and with a deeply moving sense of gratitude. But I also talk with a certain amount of impertinence and even rage. For the church is my home, and my faith is really a family matter.

I would like to say that like others who have lived through and written about the same sort of experiences that I have "I, too, believe in justice and hope!" After all, when all our reasonings have been laid to rest, all of us really believe in the same things. We're not like that group of Sundayschool children whose teacher prepared them for the bishop's visit by having each of them memorize a separate article of the creed. When "His Excellency" got there, he decided to follow a far less pedagogical and realistic method (a failing frequently noted among bishops). "You there," said the bishop, pointing to Louie in the second row, "What comes right after 'I believe in God?'" Joey, who sat at the back of the church, rushed to the aid of the hierarchy and shouted: "Excuse me, Mr. Bishop, but the guy who believes in God is Johnny, in the front row!"

As you go through the book, you will note that I have included several passages from my diary. I did this, partly, because they were already written, but mainly because they provided me with a readymade means of serving up some "daily bread," warm and fresh from the oven.

You will also note that this book is riddled with Brazilianisms, most of which can readily be grasped from context.

On this occasion I want to say that I am happy to have lived all I have at the banquet of life. After all, by the time we get to the dessert, we will realize that the whole thing has been pure grace. As an appetizer, let me cite some salutory advice I once read in the bulletin of the Little Brothers of Charles de Foucauld: "Don't laugh at me too much for trying to walk a straight line amid the present lurchings of the church." After all, haven't I said that *I believe in hope?*

I place this book, as I do all things mine, in the already risen hands of that poor little woman of the people, the mother of Jesus Christ, the savior of mankind. She is truly blessed, because she believed with a faith that was totally free.

I

The Life
That Has Given
Meaning To My Credo

1

I was born on the banks of the "weavers' river," the Llobregat, in 1928—on a great dairy farm. (I later wrote: "A pox on all large estates, but not on the eyes of their cows.")* My family was Catholic and right-wing: the terms were synonymous in those days. On my father's side, my roots were sunk deep in the earth of "Candáliga," our ancestral farm and farmhouse. On my mother's side, I came from a long line of sharp-eyed, sharp-tongued, dynamic tradesmen.

At our house, they were always talking about Gil Robles and the CEDA. In our parish, they were always talking about Fejocisme and Avant-guardisme.**

Those were the days of "benevolent dictatorship," when law and order were ipso facto the common good.

---

*"Latifundio," a term meaning a huge, landed estate, is one of Casaldáliga's bugbears. In Spain, the problem of the "latifundios" pertains not so much to Catalonia, where he was born, as to the South. But in Brazil, Casaldaliga's bitterest battles have been waged with the "latifundios."
**Fejocisme and Avant-guardisme were part of the Catalonian movement for Catholic Action. Fejocisme was for members who were sixteen or over; Avant-guardisme was for those under that age.

The revolution of 1936 caught me in the Red Zone. My Uncle Luis, a priest, and two of his companions, were killed by the Reds near Mas Lladó, just before they reached a providential hiding-place. In *Autobiographical Memoirs of an Aspiring Journalist,* I wrote:

At the ripe old age of eight, the war attracted me to its inexorable school of advanced journalism. With the coming of the war, I learned to listen carefully to my elders, who were always making sage observations on very grave matters. I also learned to adopt their habit of suddenly growing silent. In my father's ancestral home, where my Uncle Josepet (the "hero") and his family were then living, I often had to hold my tongue in front of the militiamen, drunk with wine and questions concerning such matters as the whereabouts of the nuns who taught me in my first school, the hiding-place of "deserters" and "draft-dodgers," or any news concerning this or that priest or friar who had changed his name or had started wearing a different kind of clothes.

I also learned to ask questions. Why, for example, did I have to go out to deliver milk at night and in the cold, when there were plenty of grownups who could do a better job of it? Why did we always have to keep the shutters closed? Why were the grownups always whispering about things we had always discussed openly before? And, finally, why was this whole mess lasting so long?

I was out of school during the week, because the school was coed and atheistic, and because the schoolmistress, a socialist, was—in my mother's summary and trenchant judgment—a "sow." On Sundays I couldn't go to Mass or catechism, not to mention the public movies, which were as off-limits for me as the coed school. So my cousins and my friends and I formed a sort of premature "gang," which ran wild over all the hills and gullies in the countryside, climbing fruit trees and exploring the two old "Moorish" castles that overlooked the town. All of these pirate excursions, as well as my prolonged stays at our family houses of "Candáliga" and "El Cortés del Pi," awakened in me an unshakable love for nature, free and untrammeled. One of the saddest images from those days often cames back to haunt me like the remorse of a murderer: the sight of a tree that we accidentally burnt down. I mention this to give you some idea of the deep pain I felt when I first came to Mato Grosso and saw the vast tracts of forest that the great landed estates had burnt off to clear the land.

During the war I went to confession in the oddest places—stables and mine-shafts—and attended many a "Mass of the catacombs." Among the pine groves I would follow the reports of the Nationalist Party which various "deserters" used to listen to on their clandestine crystal sets. And when the Nationalists entered my town in 1939—after our bridges had been blown up and my uncle's flock, together with my little gray goat, had been carried off—I greeted them wildly, with a sweet sense of revenge for the three years of oppressive silence I had had to live through.

We brought the remains of my martyred uncle to the town cemetery. Later on, my mother made a little embroidered pouch of green cloth, containing a tooth of the good priest, and hung it around my neck as a relic.

The war was over at last.

I was now an altar boy, officially and publicly.

In the midst of her ceaseless knitting and her endless mumble of Ave Marias, my Grandmother Francisca (the skin of her hand was as warm and smooth as a breast) would look up and ask me: "Why don't you become a priest, Pedro?" I would always answer: "Because no, Grandma. Leave me alone." And the rest of my elders would add, discreetly: "Yes, leave the boy alone." Nevertheless, the old lady (who is now in heaven), and my martyred uncle the priest, and all those "deserters" who died tragically in concentration camps, had all promised me some exceptional gift after the war was over. I thought it might be one of those little "Pate-Baby" movie cameras. What they actually gave me was the first stirrings of my vocation.

One drizzly autumn afternoon, I stood looking through the panes of our balcony window. Witnesses to the scene were two geraniums on the balcony and the hermitage of La Mare de Déu del Castell on the horizon. My mother was cleaning her room and I was in the kitchen straightening up a cupboard drawer. It was a Saturday, the day we always had a coffee-cake and that special kind of chocolate that was so different from our everyday "Arumí" brand. It was an ideal day for sharing confidences.

I, who prided myself in being a reactionary—since that meant, in the parlance of my elders, one who belonged to the opposition—was nostalgically singing the Falangist song of the Flechas (Arrows). "Take to the sky, arrow of Spain, for you must find your mark. Search out that imperial state which will carry you through sky and earth and sea. . . ."

I went into my parents' room—that place of frequent, mysterious goings-on—and, to my mother's surprise, I threw my arms around her neck and burst into tears. "Mother, I want to be a priest!"

I studied my first year of Latin at home, under the direction of our parish priest, out of an old "Miguel" grammar that was yellow with dirt and age. The following summer I entered the seminary at Vich, where my uncle had studied. More exactly, it was the new seminary of La Gleva, on the banks of the River Ter. That was a dull and trying year, but it served to clinch my priestly vocation, of which I was fully aware, for all my immaturity. During this period I sang many of the songs of the great romantic poet of Catalonia, Jacint Verdaguer. At this time, too, I also launched my first verses upon the public: poems defending Menresa against the arrogance of the citizens of Igualada. When I arrived home for vacations, I announced: "I will be a poet." And I know that my father was secretly moved at the announcement, for he bore within him the bits and pieces of many aborted vocations, ever since the time he spent two years in the seminary—at Vich.

"The silences of my father and his crippled hopes," and the fifteen years of Parkinson's disease that eventually brought him to his death (at which he was assisted by me, his priestly son), left a deep mark on me. My father's life had been spent in deep shadows. He worked hard. During my mother's illness, he would do whatever household task was required of him. He was often silent. Some nights, after tending to the cows, he would go (as an escape?) to the movies. He followed the political columns of "El Correo Catalán," and commented at length on them, above all with one close friend whom I still remember as an emblem of their friendship. And then I saw him dead, still young, still tall and handsome, with a full beard, like that of some saint.

In the seminary, a small number of us used to play at being missionaries—the real kind, persecuted and martyred. It was a seminary version of "cops and robbers." These games of ours, our visits to the tomb of St. Anthony Claret in Vich, and our conspiratorial conversations (somewhat disdainful of our "secular" superiors), eventually led me to the crowning point in my priestly vocation: I would become a missionary.

"You'll what?" asked my mother. "Think it over carefully," added my father, soberly. "Let him be," dogmatized my Uncle Jaime, the greatest tradesman in the Pla clan. "When that boy says something . . . when he wants it. . . ."

My mother said goodbye to me in the street, before we reached the station. My father accompanied me to Cervera de la Segarra, near the former university, so reminiscent of Philip II and so very Claretian. Within a short month I moved to Alagón: Alagón with its dust and its River Ebro, with its beehives of Castellar and its islet in the middle of the river. I was outside Catalonia, in the great world away from home. Then I went to Barbastro, to the novitiate, to Vich again, then to Solsona and Valls. In 1952, on the occasion of the Eucharistic Congress at Barcelona, I was ordained a priest on the lawn of the Olympic Stadium of Montjuich, by the saintly archbishop of La Paz, Abel Antezana.

Concerning my "years of formation," I could say much the same that others have said in numerous books and reviews. Because all the novitiates and seminaries in the world were much the same in those long-gone, obscurantist, and heroic days.

Of those years of my "studies"—humanities, philosophy, and theology—I have the fondest memories of classmates now scattered throughout the world. Friends with whom I shared the crises of youth, of obedience and of more or less lucid studies; with whom I discussed the church and the Claretian congregation; with whom I plotted a revolution "from the inside." I have the same fond memories of my teachers and directors, some of whom were sometimes mistaken, though nearly all of them were generous; some of whom, providentially, changed my grades.

As for cultural, artistic, and creative projects, or involvements in movements dedicated to a more "committed" spirituality, or apostolic endeavors—I was into them all. I founded and directed a number of school reviews (all of which appeared in a single issue); I wrote sketches and began to think seriously and apostolically about the press, the radio, and films. More than once, during those deep vocational confidences that punctuate and light up so many hours of seminary routine, I informed my classmates of my unshakable resolve to be a writer. More than once, also, I had the feeling that the life ministry of a writer was a bit too secular. Literature had a bad reputation among our spiritual directors. I remember, concretely, bidding poetry farewell on many sad occasions, as one bids an impossible girlfriend farewell.

I "officially" renounced Catalán, because it was expedient that we all adopt "one" language. Later on, I would have to renounce Castilian, too, in favor of Portuguese. Or, to put it less dramatically, I was stuck with three sister-languages, each of which I was unsure of at different times and in different measure. This always brings on a kind of castration-complex for anyone who has chosen words as his forte. (All of this, even though it might not seem so at first, forms part of my faith, which has always complicated my life with its consequences.)

"Piety," "duty," "mortification," "ideals," "perfection"—

all these words filled my spiritual notebooks and involved me in a sincere and sometimes brutal effort during my seminary years.

I learned to meditate on the things of God. I learned to pray much, although I still don't know how well. I learned to love the Blessed Virgin, sentimentally and mariologically. During my years of philosophical studies, I discovered the mystery of Jesus Christ in the Bible, and more particularly in St. Paul. During my theological studies, I discovered the paschal eucharist. I also discovered, somewhat to my dazzlement, the hope-giving horizons of eschatology. And I began to glimpse—just to glimpse—something of the meaning of the church.

I had always wanted to go to the missions, but I believe that it was not until Monsignor Fogued, the prefect apostolic of Tunki in China (an Aragonese through and through who had become a somewhat mythical figure to us because of his beard and his word), that I made "the" option for "the missions"—an option which I staunchly held to and which led me eventually to Mato Grosso.

It was also during those delicious days of my studies when I began to beg for martyrdom, as one begs for a place in the front ranks.

The world was evil. Outside the church there was no salvation. And zeal—that mixture of temperament, formation, and grace—was burning me up. The definition of a Claretian missionary, which Anthony Claret had left us as a legacy, begged for just that: "A man on fire with love, who sets its fire wherever he goes. . . ."

In my twenty-fourth year, beneath the flames of Pentecost and summer, I celebrated my first, nervously happy Mass, in the sacristy of the Shrine of the Immaculate Heart of Mary in Barcelona. And, after twelve long years of absence, I returned to my home and my town, as a priest.

2

My first "temporary" assignment was to last for six years, in Sabadell. Because my superiors needed me, they cut short my "pastoral year" at Baltar in Galicia, that prow of land that juts into the surf and joins the green of Cantabria and the Atlantic, there in that Land's End, and sent me to the "salt mines" of a school for boys.

Sabadell was my first love in the ministry, the first place in which many aspects of my life were forged. Old Sabadell, with its textile factories, its endless streets, its barracks at Can Oriach, Can Puiggener, and Torre Romeu. Sabadell, with its "Murcian" families, its apprentice boys, its world of workers and migrants. Sabadell, with its grueling hours of classes, confessions, and unprepared counseling; with the noise and clatter of its offices and floors; with its aged Marian Sodalists and its modern, "excommunicated" cursillistas.

All those hasty dinners of cold cauliflower, after ten hours of classes, or after three long hours of shared, excessive confidences. All those radio scripts written at 2:00 A.M. in the silent sacristy. The inevitable breviary, which I used to say while pacing back and forth in the refectory before 1:00 A.M.—where I often woke up abruptly while leaning against the wall. Those intense nights of clausuras, with my mind a blank. Then there were those violent attacks of sleepiness where I slumped asleep right there in front of the watchful young eyes of my students. The friendships and ties I formed as "father of the street urchins." The review, *Euphoria,* which I and a group of daring young men founded and directed. It died after its eighth issue, broke but unblemished. That mixed bag of a community, which was as sincere as it was artificial and impossible. My first loneliness as a young priest. Our blind will to reform the congregation, the church, and the world.

From Sabadell I was sent to Barcelona, once again, to a hopelessly heterogeneous community, with its school, its church, the provincial house, and its youth work. And in Barcelona I experienced most completely, most universally and brutally, the human experience of migration, work, family, so-called society, vice, remorse, sorrow, and illusion. I discovered the masses in Barcelona, in its crowded subway, in its factories and streets. Through the offices of the Juventud Claretiana which I ran at 365 Nápoles Street, there was a nightly parade—which caused some conflicts of obedience and made me lose many meals and much peace—of "suspicious" people: bearded old men, young malcontents, pregnant or very attractive women, workers on strike or without housing, sick people without money, hungry kids, loiterers, con artists, and delinquents. Others used to sleep, eat pitifully, and do all kinds of washing in the adjoining theater. Thanks to this parade of people, this translation of celluloid into flesh and blood, I and the "normal" young people I directed came to a much better understanding of some of the socially oriented movies we saw in our Cine Forum.

While I was in Barcelona I kept up my contacts with the cursillo movement which was now split down the middle into two separate groups: the original movement, which was "free," and the more clerical or hierarchical movement, which was being used as a tool of Catholic Action. I also wrote a weekly Marian program for radio, which was broadcast by eleven second-class stations. The scripts would later serve as the basis for a book in the "Cosas de Dios" (The Things of God) series. This book, entitled *Our Lady of the Twentieth Century*, had some wonderful illustrations by Francisco Izquierdo. I also worked on *University '61, The Other Cinema*, and still other reviews. I also wrote some poems, a vocational novel, and a collective autobiography of the seminary courses I had gone through.

While I was in Barcelona I was called to establish the cursillo movement in Africa, in that Guinea which was then called "Spanish." I worked with Eduardo Bonnin, with Vidal and with Casas, three very dear names among the hundreds of unforgettable names that the cursillos engraved on my life.

Those were heady times, partly because of the uprisings in the Belgian Congo, which were the first painful symptoms of the "awakening of Africa." We gave "mixed" cursillos, to blacks and whites, against the respectable opinion of some of the most honored colonizers of the place. We stuck to our guns and used to say: "either coffee with cream, or nothing!" I felt Africa, colonized and catechized, physically, like the blast of tropical air that hit my lungs in the whitewashed airport of Nigeria, which looked so composed beneath the all too peaceful "Pax Britannica." I had a mad sense of the reality and the call of the Third World. And when I came back to Spain on the vigil of the Epiphany (dressed ridiculously, for that time of year in Madrid, in a white cassock), I bore within me, like a fetus, the vague but powerful notion of Africa, the Third World, the poor of the earth, and the new church—the church of the poor—of which we would talk so much later, with the coming of Vatican II.

A half-year later, in 1961, after three years of ministry in

Barcelona, I had bought my ticket on Iberia airlines and was all set to return to Guinea, when a new "assignment" arrived: I was to make an about-face and head for Barbastro, as prefect of the Claretian seminary. I had to catch the "renfe" and, on the last leg of my journey, the pathetic little narrow-gauged train, the "Burreta," and there I was, in charge of the Claretian seminarians in their senior courses in humanities, there in that corner of Huesca, almost in the folds of the Aragonese Pyrenees, leeward of "El Pueyo," of the olive and almond trees of Our Lady, and overshadowed by the still-living memory of my fifty-some Claretian brethren who were martyred there in 1936.

The almost obsessive restrictions and responsibilities of a formation director—I had to be an example to all the students—together with the lonely quiet of that big old house on Calle Conde, and the shabbiest house imaginable in post-Tridentine Spain, made the whole experience a second novitiate for me, one that was much more consciously lived than the first, and no less austere and impassioned. I returned to intense prayer, to "fidelity in small matters," to cilices and disciplines, and to nightly vigils and fasts. But I also had to risk some changes and revisions in the molds of religious and apostolic life, to bring them into line with a greater commitment to practice. For I was a director of formation, and an iconoclastic one, at that. Right away I burnt up all the plastic flowers in the seminary. I took down a number of the saints who were cluttering up the little altar in the chapel and, once again in conflict with my superiors (poor, patient, Virgilian Father Mir!), I revolutionized timetables, customs, prayers, readings, guidelines, and perspectives.

The good days of Vatican II had arrived. The daybooks

and notices on the Council, the heartening interventions from the floor, the free opinions of the *periti,* what the Council *was* in fact, and what it *could* be for the future of the church—all these things filled me with a wild sense of enthusiasm and gratitude.

While I was camping out with some of my seminarians in the Pyrenees, I received a new assignment: to go to Madrid as director of the centenary Cordimarian publication, the "Iris de Paz." A terrible and maddening assignment. In Madrid, it is true, I could do so many things: in the press, the cursillo movement, among the black university students from Guinea, and in all those underworlds I had become familiar with in Sabadell and Barcelona. I kept on dreaming, for the time being, and obeyed with my usual automatic precision. Of course, as the subdirector general of the congregation remarked, I was really a man of "genuine accomplishments," who had always come off with A's, when all the rest were getting B's.

I dedicated the first issue of the review (before it was subjected to the renewal I planned for the coming year), to "Our Lady of the Guardia Civil." It was October, the feast of El Pilar, and God knows what other anniversary of the Blessed Virgin. It so happened that, wherever I had been—in Guinea, in Huesca and, later on, in Madrid— through the cursillo movement and interminable chains of friends of friends of friends, I ended up being a great friend of the "cops," almost a sort of super-official "Padre," and even an "honorary lieutenant," because of the gangs of young troublemakers I had converted in Bata. I was friends with a number of militiamen, too, for the same reasons. How close and yet how contradictory these friendships seem to me, now that I have become an ogre to the police, as I shall try to explain.

I irreverently stripped the old review of all its trappings, leaving hardly an "Iris" behind, and added the boastful subtitle: "A Review of Witness and Hope." I attacked the forces of tradition, within and without, because of the new format, the new drawings, the new subject-matter and the new criteria which I adopted. And I finally brought down upon my head the wrath of my superiors in Rome, in the form of a letter of dismissal from my post, because of an article in which I referred to some social pronouncement of the Spanish bishops as "a disappointing declaration."

In connection with the review and with other activities in Madrid, a group of close Claretian companions—friends from former times, who have grown in friendship ever since, and with whom I have shared a life of total communion—was formed. These "soul-brothers" and companions in decisive moments, an association of fellow-travelers that I cannot do without, included Fernando Sebastián, Teófilo Cabestrero, Maximino Cerezo Barredo, Santi, Velasco, and a few more.

In Madrid I became fully involved in the cursillo movement. I was even named national counselor. The conflict between the two parties, which I mentioned earlier (there were actually three), had become even more deeply polarized. The hierarchy was doing its utmost to shape new guidelines for the movement by main force, while the original cell from Mallorca—which I considered to be the legitimate mother of the movement—was almost under interdict. Notwithstanding all this, I had plenty of opportunities within Madrid and outside it, within the cursillo movement and outside it. It was at this time, in cursillos, clausuras, ultreyas, spiritual direction and other contacts, that I attracted a large constellation of friends who have helped and upheld this mission and its bishop with moving fidelity. The parlors at Buen Suceso 22 were filled every evening, under the austere and watchful eye of Brother Mallas, the porter; a new, small experimental community, in the style of Vatican II, was opened by Teófilo and me on Pasaje Lóriga 10, under the thought-provoking, gray pictures by Cerezo; and Castelló 57, Apt. 1, was the priestly counseling room where innumerable confidences were shared, evening after evening, soul after soul, in the same presumptuous and motified style as at Sabadell, Barcelona, and Barbastro.

This went on until one day, when six companions, Claretians and rebels—writers from Madrid, professors at Salamanca—got together and decided to write an ultimatum to the superior general of the congregation, the ever-understanding Father Schweiger, who sometime earlier had characterized me as an impenitent "vir desideriorum." We insisted that either the congregation should accept Vatican II or we would have to try following some new course of action. I remember our signing that letter in the quixotic shadow of the editorial offices of the "Iris de Paz," and how we felt like people signing a request for a leave of absence or a revolutionary manifesto. And Father Schweiger answered us with Teutonic seriousness, and with an ecclesial sense of responsibility that was equal to any test. On his way back from Latin America, where he had received our letter, he went out of his way to pass through Madrid and meet with us. And he assured us that he was one with us in the intention of seeing to it that the Claretian congregation—in its next general chapter—should in fact accept the legacy of Vatican II.

The General Chapter of Renewal was held in Rome, toward the end of 1967. I was summoned to participate in it as the representative of the province of Aragón. It was a hard-fought battle—honest, pious, sullen, juridical, charismatic—between the opposing factions of the Claretian congregation, and it sustained a climate of Celtiberic passion throughout the placid, Roman *ottobrata* at the house on Via Aurelia. The room where our younger group met and plotted came to be called the "Sierra Maestra," and I soon inherited the compromising title of "Che Guevara." In sober fact, during that general chapter, the clear meaning of the Claretian chapter was keenly felt, and I think that all of us, young and not so young, left it somewhat marked by a renewed religious and apostolic life. Our mission in the church was to "proclaim the Word." We had to *live* Vatican II. The time had come when we must renew or die.

It was during this Chapter of Renewal that I decided in favor of Mato Grosso. For me, too, an hour of decision had arrived. I have mentioned Che Guevara: he had just died, and his lay testimony was one more call to me from America. For a while I had been undecided whether to go to Bolivia or Brazil, because an Indian mission in the high plains of Bolivia had been asking for some missionary volunteers, and Bolivia always seemed to be the last place that was always left behind. It was Father Schweiger himself who helped me decide for Brazil. The Holy See, through the nunciature in Rio, had been asking the Claretian congregation for four years—seeing that they had done so well in missioning the central region of Goiás—to take care of the unattended northern stretches of the Mato Grosso.

I had been freed from the threat of being made provincial of Aragón. I accepted this new permission and commitment to found a Claretian mission in Mato Grosso. And so, on January 26, 1968, Manuel and I left the 11 degrees below zero (Celsius) of Madrid and were hit by the blast of

28 degrees above zero at Galeão Airport in Rio de Janeiro. It was a leap into the void of another world. I had finally attained what I had dreamed and prayed and sought for, rabidly, throughout all the days of my vocation: "the missions"—a heroic climate where I could live heroically. I used to say that back then, when I was naive and stubborn, and—who knows?—perhaps faithful.

3

Brazil was then living in the full light of the glorious revolution of '61, with some of the more heated characteristics of the revolution of '68. The CENFI—Center for Intercultural Formation—with its sixty missionaries, men and women of different nationalities and the most diverse backgrounds, was a cauldron of clashing freedoms. Everything was being revised; everyone was living in a state of criticism. From the "New-Church" Dutch group, with its spontaneous liturgies and its fractious attitude toward the Vatican, through the Brazilian professors of the CENFI, eclectic laymen or "secularized" clerics (as they seemed at first sight to a Spanish Claretian), to the solid Bretons, still saying Mass in Latin, one could run the whole spiritual gamut of a church that was evolving, both in Latin America and in Brazil.

So many memorable events filled the program at CENFI. There were, for example, the lectures of Father Luis Segundo . . . chats with university students who had been veterans of the early, daring youth movements . . . visits to different places, such as the Volta Redonda of Dom Valdir, the *fazendas* of the Rio valley, the *favelas* . . . selected plays and movies, such as *Morte e Vida Severina*, to cite but one that I found particularly moving . . . the intoxicating sessions of Umbanda, the commentaries in the daily press, with all the remarks and hints of repression, of exposés on different "churches" in the country . . . various desacralized (!), different, "consciousness-raising" services . . . the breviary skipped, sometimes, "without sin". . . . All of this contributed to make us review and restate all the formation we had received, the piety we had inherited, the austere distance between the sexes that we had observed, our sedentary, rectory-bound ministries, the ease with which we of the "Old World" had allowed ourselves to be convinced of the necessity for maintaining the dichotomy between the mission of the church and politics and society in general.

Those four months at CENFI, in the autumn of our transition from Europe to America, were an abrupt and salutary novitiate in secularization and in forward-looking criticism. It was daring, yes, but useful. To have come to Mato Grosso directly from Europe, without passing through CENFI, would have been a fatal plunge for us. At the very least, we would not have had an informed perspective of Brazil and the Brazilian church.

After CENFI, we spent a month and a half in the monstrous city of São Paulo. We visited hospitals and the reptile center at Butantã, where we took a mini-course in tropical diseases and hazards. This provided us with a set of anticipated fantasies of all the possible ills which the Amazon could never inflict upon any human being at one time, but which it would eventually visit upon us one by one, daily. Those weeks immediately preceding our arrival at the mission involved a heroic degree of availability. We began our trek towards the unknown West. Seven days by truck from Rio Claro in São Paolo to the banks of the Araguaia, with the faith of Abraham. (Some days later, as I

read Deiss' *Mary, Daughter of Sion,* I became confirmed in
the basically detached attitude of the patriarch of all those
who go out in search of a land and mission to which the
Lord has directed them.)

That was in July of 1968. We arrived in a world from
which there was no turning back. The mission consisted of
150,000 square kilometers of rivers, plains, and forest, located in the northwest corner of Mato Grosso, in so-called
"legal" Amazonia, between the Araguaia and Xingu Rivers, but including the "Ilha do Bananal," the largest mid-
river island in the world. The only "church-base" we had
was our four-by-eight house on the banks of the marvelous
and muddy Araguaia. We didn't know where to begin or
even where anybody lived in the region—which is so vast
and full of distances of all sorts that it provided us with all
the ready-made excuses for indecision we could use. The
only road (which we had traveled on to get here) was just
opening up, with its dusty-red tracks cutting a swath
through the forest and cleared patches, where the small
tiger called the *onça* was at full liberty to block our path as
it bounded before us.

There wasn't a single doctor in the area. There was no
mail, no electric light, no telephone, no telegraph. In all of
São Félix there were three old jeeps, the only cars in the
whole place. The best qualified schoolmistress was a
"well-endowed" black woman who had had a year and a
half of grammar school training, was often drunk, and had
given many classes in her little grass shack of a school with
armed guards posted outside to protect her from the
jaguars and the Indians.

I began my diary for August 15th: "Here, perhaps—in
the midst of these great silences—I'm going to need to
resort to interior dialogue more than ever before.... We

arrived in this mission on July 30th, and I have thought and felt and feared and hoped for and enjoyed many things. Men, nature, God. . . ."

Those first months Manuel and I acted as medics, thumbing our way blindly through lists of "counter-indications." And we witnessed firsthand the multiple, enslaving presence of sickness and death in the region: worms, dehydration, malaria, hepatitis, umbilical tetanus, all sorts of skin disease, and the chronic illness of malnutrition. During the first week of our stay in São Félix four children died. Placed in cardboard boxes, like pairs of shoes, they were carried from their houses, en route to that little cemetery by the river. That little cemetery where we would have to bury so many children (each family can count on three or four dying) and so many adults (who either died natural deaths or were killed)—some nameless, some without even a coffin.

I wrote in my diary:

These people listen. Sometimes they smile. Nearly always, they are silent. How distant my words seem to be from their simple, elemental soul, hardened by suffering and total neglect!

These people are drifters: a people who come and go on the winds of poverty, loneliness, their own crimes or those of others. . . . (The collective crime of social injustice!) Simple people, people carrying a cross. . . . These people are—whatever might be said to the contrary—the poor of the gospel.

We were forced to totally overhaul our preconceived criteria and programs. Where should we begin? What were the people looking for? What could we do about it? What did it really mean to "be a church" here?

We had a little mud hut of a church, which was at the mercy of the tornadoes. There was a great deal of superstition. Then there was the time-honored custom of the *desobrigas* or Easter-duty visits which the oldtime Padres used to make in the north and central West, where most of our settlers had come from. We couldn't get out of making these *desobrigas* during the first year and a half of our mission. It took us that long to get to know the terrain and the people which had been entrusted to us as our priestly inheritance. And we had to do this, even though we had no use for these "courtesy visits"—which were always surrounded by a hundred and one animals, three-hundred people, hasty weddings, baptisms and confessions, girls raped, drunken brawls, confrontations, gunshots. . . .

It was during these *desobrigas* that we began to sense the problem of *land.* Nobody had his own land. Nobody had an assured future. Everyone was a *retirante,* an emigrant from other parts of the country that had already been eaten up by the *latifundio*—the great, landed estate-companies. Bands of them kept streaming in from the northwest and the north, with their eight or ten children in tow, looking for "open" land without an owner, until one day they crossed the Araguaia, as if they were crossing the Red Sea into the Promised Land.

Pontinópolis ("Bridgeville"). All over again. The living sensation of poverty, abandonment, human injustice, the necessary (if unverifiable) providence of God for all his poor children of the earth.

I was impressed to learn how most of these people, who came from Maranhao, Pará, Ceará, and from the North in general, had left their lands in search of a mythical "green strip" of land which had been prophesied to them, some thirty or more years earlier,

by their great seer, Padre Cícero Romao, of Juazeiro do
Norte, in Ceará. This man—demagogue, fanatic, prophet, or what have you—the revered "Padrinho" and Moses
of so many northeasterners who had been scourged by
drought and misery, had prophesied hard days, irrepa-
rable droughts, hunger.... For the northeasterners, inhabitants of a heartless region that has been touchingly
portrayed in a few Brazilian films, all these "prophecies"
were easy enough to believe, since they had been confirmed by constant past experiences. The "green strip"
would be the jungle, the green forest of the Mato Grosso,
of Amazonia.... And thus began the long caravan of
retirantes who are now our mission, the people we live
among, and for whom, Lord, one would wish to die ...
(*Diary*, September 12th).

Mato Grosso was, and still is, a land without law. Someone has dubbed it the "fluid state" of Brazil. There is no
administrative substructure, no labor organization, no fis-
cal system. "The Law" was the strongest or most brutal.
Money and a 38 were what got things done. "To be born,"
"to die," "to kill": these three were both the most basic laws
and the most frequently conjugated verbs—all three of
them done and spoken of with chilling nonchalance.

The county seat of São Félix is, to this day, 700 kilometers away, in Barra do Garças. Sometimes it seems we don't
exist....

Illiteracy was the rule, and the education of children—
which conjured up visions of a future escape from the sad
fate of their parents—was of even greater concern to the
people than their right to own land or to eat. From the first
moment of our arrival, the petitions poured in: would we
give classes, would we build a school, would we organize a

boarding school, could we take care of orphans, adopt them, educate them. . . ? They had no idea that a couple of Padres or Sisters couldn't even begin to tackle such a vast problem.

In fact, the need was so great that—with financial help from friends in Spain—we did manage, with great love and suffering, to build a secondary school, the *Ginásio Estadual Araguaia*. It would belong to the state and the people, because neither the Claretians nor the prelature wanted to own any buildings here. We would assume responsibility for its direction and staff, and we would make the school into a totally "different" center of formation. . . .

Young lay people, girls and boys, began to arrive at the mission—as teachers. They were followed by a community of Sisters of St. Joseph. (In the northern area of the prelature, in the village of the Tapirapé Indians near Santa Terezinha, there was a community of the Little Sisters of Jesus. They had been there for fifteen years, but their vocation was one of presence, of just being there, of becoming incarnate in the native poverty and culture of the Indians, as a gospel witness.)

We also simply had to face the public health problem. We transformed the little house on the river bank into a walk-in clinic. The nursing sisters would have an ample field for the practice of charity.

In Santa Terezinha, which at that time belonged to the prelature of Conceição do Araguaia, Fr. Francisco Jentel was attending to the needs of the *posseiros* (squatters) and the Tapirapé Indians. São Félix, Santa Terezinha, and Tapirapé were to become the three unique missionary communities belonging to the prelature that was created in 1970.

In April of 1971, when the rains were over (the year,

which is always hot, is divided in half between a rainy and a "dry" season), and the rice was being harvested (rice is our daily bread here) and, liturgically, we were celebrating Easter, we began a new pastoral experiment: missionary campaigns. They were to take the place of the old *desobrigas*. They were something like popular missions, but were held on the bare ground. They called for three months of teamwork in a given place, with classes in the ABCs (according to Paulo Freire's method), with weekly Masses geared to the mentality of the people (more like catechesis or evangelization than a eucharist!), and preparation for baptism and the other sacraments, with a growing awareness of the lived reality of daily life, the discovery of local leaders, and the cultivation of some leaven for future communities.

We celebrated the first of these missionary campaigns in Pontinópolis, a settlement some 125 kilometers distant from São Félix. It was during this campaign that we were definitely recognized as being on the side of the *posseiros*, or squatters, hounded from state to state by the latifundios. It was during these missionary campaigns that we, too, firmly grasped the problematic of our people: the basic social conflict in a region officially slated to be a latifundio for cattle raising (part of the Superintendency for the Development of Amazonia—SUDAM), where cowdung is like an official seal of "national integration," and where Indians, *posseiros* and peons begin their inhuman disintegration.

4

In September of 1970, I had already drawn up an exposé-report on the state of slavery in which perhaps a third of the population of our prelature were living: the

peoes, beasts of burden, manual laborers enticed fraudu-
lently from the northern and central sections of the country, and then dumped here to do piecework and planting
of these infinite *fazendas* which, with their hundreds of
thousands of hectares of land, are really concentration
camps. The report was entitled: "Slavery or Feudalism in
Northern Mato Grosso." I sent it to the top government
authorities, to the Presidency of the National Council of
Bishops, and to the Apostolic Nunciature. The nuncio,
after diplomatically praising my pastoral courage and
realism, proceeded to request, diplomatically, that I
should not allow it to be published abroad, since this would
only assist the chorus of defamation that foreigners were
already orchestrating against Brazil. . . .

> *Diary* 2/9/70: I have just finished my "report" on
> Feudalism and Slavery in Northern Mato Grosso. I hope
> that the Spirit of Jesus will give it the ring of truth and
> love that I myself can't give it. I know that these themes
> set me on fire and infuriate me. . . .

The report was little more than a tragic litany of life-
and-blood cases of peons who had been deceived, controlled at gunpoint, beaten, wounded or killed, fenced-in
in the forest, in total disregard for the law, without any
rights, without any human way out.

It was a moonlit night when I signed that document. I
went out to look at the moon and take in some of the
cooler air outside, and I offered myself to the Lord. I felt
that in signing that document, I may have signed my own
death warrant. In any case, I had just signed a challenge.

Sure enough, a few days later I received a bit of advice
from one of the greatest landholders (or "landgrabbers")
in Brazil—the first of many company-owned, ecclesiastical,

"friendly" warnings: I shouldn't get mixed up in things like this, otherwise people would begin accusing me of being a subversive.... It was really the federal police who were controlling us.... The Lieutenant Delegate of São Félix was an agent.... The *Fazendeiros* were going to institute proceedings against me, etc.

We had now made a clean break with the *fazendas*. We could no longer celebrate the eucharist under the shelter of these lords of the earth. No more traveling in their cars or airplanes, no more sharing food or whiskey at their tables, no more being "assisted" at Mass by those who were systematically enslaving their lesser brothers. That was no longer the Lord's Supper! We were losing the friendship of the great and facing up to them. No exploiter or profiteer from exploitation could be a godparent at a baptism, for example. We stopped accepting rides from them, we positively shunned their company and their smiles. We even ceased greeting the most barefaced offenders. (On the other hand, we were winning the trust and love of the poor and the oppressed.) It was an hour of decision and choice—a heartrending choice that did violence to my own temperament, to my natural desire to be on good terms with everyone, to my evangelical training in "meekness," to the venerable pastoral norm of "not quenching the smoking flax." It was a tearing experience that still adds to the tension of the cross of my life.

5

Throughout these latest years of the "life that has given meaning to my credo," I am taking the liberty of transcribing some pages from the diary that I have been sketching ever since I arrived here in Mato Grosso—sometimes they will seem sparse, sometimes crammed, sometimes as monotonous as life. These pages seem more spontaneous and true to me than anything I might concoct in hindsight. They illumine the circumstances and motivations that enveloped me during these dark hours. They say a little about everything and thus, in passing, they speak of my faith in God, in Christ, in the church, in man, in the world. And of my faith in justice and in hope.

Two journalists—one of them from the *Los Angeles Times*—interview me on the scandals at Codeara and other *fazendas* hereabouts, which have recently made the front page of papers in this country. I speak to them without much care about being discreet. The reporter from the *Times*—who informs me that he is a Catholic—tells me (alas, all too correctly!) that the church is the only voice that can speak out in Brazil today, to denounce these injustices. He adds: history will judge of this in the future . . . (2/3/71).

One regular day, September 22, 1970, I wrote:

Around ten this morning they brought in a woman from the Island, who had died Sunday, of malaria. . . . A half-hour later I was told of the death of a peon who had been shot to ribbons by our new Sargento Edson, of the military police. . . .
We had just buried an unknown. "He's from Ceara," said the Captain—by way of total identification. "You act like you've never had to bury anyone," said one gravedigger to another who seemed uneasy about the business. (Has anyone *not* been a gravedigger here?)
Yesterday, at the "Tres Marias," one peon ran another through with a knife.
There is more dying and killing than there is living.

Here it is easier, more within ones means, to die and kill, than it is to live.

As I am writing these lines, a foreman from Suiá-Missu (not just some anonymous peon) comes in, his eye gouged out by a branch. *The Fazenda*, the almighty Fazenda, with a capital "f," the greatest cattle ranch in Latin America, put a few drops of ointment in his eye, refused to sign a letter of recommendation for him, and let him go—him and his eight children. . . .

10/1/70: At dinner we talked about companies, about FUNAI (the Foundation for the Indian), about official Brazil. The topic pains us. Where is this mission headed? What future can these people hope for? Where can we start, prophetically and humbly?

I read where some communist writer said: "Either love is political or it does not exist." I would agree, but I would add: "*Either it is total* (yes! for the whole man, for everyman, for heaven and earth!) *or it is not.* . . .

In Furo das Pedras, on the 12th, the feast of Our Lady of the Vision, I had a good pastoral encounter with those simple folks. We also encountered CODEARA (Company for the Development of the Araguaria) there. Its two "lawyers"—Olimpio Jaime and the great six-shooter strapped on his thigh—were going around, trying to wheedle statements and signatures from the *posseiros* for God knows what compensation.

Today, when I arrived home at noon, I found a *posseiro* from Tapiraguaia, on the verge of tears. He had been living on his little "place" for nine years. Then, on Monday, Officer Camargo—always a great demolition man—threatened him with police action if he tried to go ahead with his planting. There was no other way out for him. He lives with his widowed mother and three little orphaned cousins.

It's clouding up, and the mosquitoes are riddling me with bites. I need a light, an entrenched fidelity, a charity that is at once committed and respectful. I am the personification of tormented powerlessness.

But everything is mission. "Faith," as Teixera-Mesters intriguingly translates the famous verse, "consists of realizing what one hopes for" (Heb 11:1) (10/14/70).

The "great ones" of Codeara and the rest of the *fazendas* in the area have gathered for a meeting and a barbecue. Today's liturgy speaks of "serving" and of "drinking the chalice" (10/18/70).

JANUARY 7, 1971:

. . . Another peon. Young. Hardly nineteen years old. Also from Codeara. He came in the day before yesterday and was buried today. He had been working at Codeara right up to the day before yesterday, and received—posthumously—a salary of a hundred miserable *cruzeiros*. A hundred pieces of silver and death. I celebrated Mass for him, with his body present, beneath our church-roof, tattered by wind and rain. Another victim of the latifundios. I would have felt little if I could have died in his place. . . .

JANUARY 31:

Yesterday afternoon at one, Antonio Barbosa, a peon, died. He was a twenty-one-year-old boy from São Miguel do Araguaia, whom Sister and Didi had brought to Santa Isabel. He died of malaria and, apparently, of typhus. We had to bury him quickly, as evening was falling.... I had wrapped him in cloths left over from making our school uniforms—cloths that had been serving as our stage curtain and backdrop. We brought Antonio to the cemetery in the jeep. An ox-driver we called "El Cearense" and two other peons accompanied us. I asked them and the gravediggers to join us in feeling as if we were the parents, brothers, sisters, and friends of that poor, abandoned boy, who was going to be buried without so much as a coffin. As I was saying the burial prayer, all the birds in the forest broke into song. All the feelings I had kept within me—anger, compassion, hope, poverty—seemed to rise chokingly to my throat, and my voice broke into sobbing. One overwhelming truth lingered on the evening air—where lowering clouds and distant lightning threatened: "I am the resurrection and the life...." I threw a little dirt on the body in the grave. I wanted to be one with Antonio, with all the peons, with all the victims of injustice in the world. Contrary to the local superstitious custom, Antonio's body was not buried facing the river. Antonio was buried facing the *fazendas*. Like an accusation. Facing the hills... and heaven, too.

February 3:

Fr. Francisco brought us some epic news. A price had been set on Fr. Henrique's head—500 cruzeiros—"the toll for a five-league stretch of road." Father's life had been bought by Officer Plinio, of the Frenova *fazenda,* whose plans for a raid had been frustrated because Fr. Henrique had tipped off the *posseiros....*

6

Santa Terezinha had for some time been the focus of conflict with the "Codeara" Company (Company for the Development of the Araguaia), run by bankers from São Paulo. The town of Serra Nova, in the Serra do Roncador, some 170 kilometers from São Félix, would become a new battleground—a battle which has not yet issued in victory, nor is the outlook very hopeful. I had pretty nearly assisted at its birth. I myself suggested the name of Serra Nova. A group of oldtime *posseiros* thereabouts had felt the need to band together in a *patrimonia,* where they could have their "business," their school, their church, their "street"—as they say very touchingly in this region of the interior. The Bordon *fazenda*—a powerful agrobusiness firm of Amazonia, which also runs a refrigerating business of the same name—with the aid of the Minister of Farms, Delfim Neto (the man responsible for the "Brazilian miracle"), as its "tour guide," had decided to cut a one and a half kilometer road through the arable land of the settlement, thus strangling forever the future of its workers. This slicing and reapportionment of land has usually signaled the outburst of some conflict. These "cuts" have been and are a source of trouble in this and other areas. On May 2, 1971, I noted in my diary:

Tiradentes. April 22. A memory of freedom and generous sacrifice.

I am in Serra Nova, the new settlement at the foot of the Serra do Roncador. It is 6:45 A.M., and I've just got to bed (rather, my hammock). I have gone "ao mata" (to the jungle), i.e., to the "natural" toilet provided by the sheltering jungle nearby the house and, on my way back, as I cross through the cornpatch, I am greeted by the clucking of Doña Luisa's startled hens. I am a guest in the first "house" in town, as you turn off from the "highway." It is Zé Raimundo's house. He and I arrived here on horseback at two in the afternoon. We had set out at a quarter after one on Monday. The first night we slept at El Maranhense's house. When we got here, night had already fallen. They were kneading dough made with mandioca flour.

It had been a seventy-five-kilometer journey, filled with impressions, meetings, notices, spectacles. Nature is a scenic marvel, here. Then there are men: suffering, courageous, hospitable.

As we traveled along the road, Zé Raimundo and I did quite a bit of talking. I learned a lot. Among other things, I learned once more that *"recurso é o trono do orgulho*—wealth is the throne of pride." And with each forward stage in our journey, I became increasingly aware of the duty, the bitterness and the unifying force of the problem of *land.* This word—land!—began to grow within me, like a crime, like a plan. It became something holy and urgent, like the gospel.

My first impression of Serra Nova was one of discovery. In the heart of the "mata," the virgin thicket— moist, alive, fruitful—a town of poor but generous people was axing its way to birth: a rural community that was fighting an uphill struggle, a community which had suffered in its own flesh the tragedy of the landless, driven from state to state, hounded by the *tiburones*—the "sharks." I visited their families. I began to enter into co-suffering with them, into their anger, into that enthusiasm which stupid men would label "subversive. . . ."

That night we gathered together—the whole town— in a large shed made of logs and thatching. The whole

thing had been put up in a single day so that, when the
Padre arrived, it could serve as the *Casa do Povo*—the
"People's House." I celebrated the first Mass in the new-
born town. There was the same sense of primitive won-
der as the Friars from the Age of Discovery must have
felt, except for the fact that many long years of the bitter
lessons of history had intervened.

The following day, some of us traveled into the forest,
to the site of the "cut" that was being opened up by a
subsidiary of the Telles surveying company. A little over
a kilometer from the settlement, this "cut" was mer-
cilessly cutting off all hope for the future. Once more,
the criminal latifundio—aided and abetted by the law
and money—was invading a new, free space that had
been a dream come true for the poor. I took down some
data. In a spirit of simplicity and camaraderie, we all
bathed in one of those limpid, cold *corregos* of the Eden-
like forest, and then arrived back at the settlement. We
had to take a stand. I would go to São Paulo or maybe,
even, Brasilia, to try to come to terms with the "sharks."
The people took heart because of my solidarity with
them, and they promised not to give up or let themselves
be intimidated. . . .

On my return to São Félix—I had had to make a de-
tour for a possible interview with one of the *fazendeiros*
involved in the case—I met Zé Maria and Vaime, who
had come to see me. Pedrito had already been trying to
spot me in his airplane around the Roncador area.
Twice. Another conflict had broken out in Santa
Terezinha. This time it was Codeara and the city hall
that had sold out to them, against the mission. . . .

I spent Monday, Tuesday, and Wednesday talking
with the "*senhores*" in São Paulo. It wasn't easy to arrange
the meetings. (It was also useless.) Besides, Senhor

Ariosto and the Superintendent Director of the Bordon Company received me so "politely," that they prevented me at every turn from getting into that dangerous area where I would start talking about land and they would start reaffirming their "rights." We ended up agreeing to talk again, before or after the famous barbecue for government ministers and *fazendeiros* that was to be held at Xingu around that time.

There were plans to allow a section of national highway BR-80 to cut through the National Indian Reservation at Xingu (and so it was, in the North, because the *fazendeiros,* who saw it as the "filet mignon" of the cattle-raising country, had a craving for it). The environmentally minded group, *Vilas Boas,* was rightly incensed over the whole affair. I think that this was the beginning of the end for any public show of concern for the preservation and protection of the Indian....

On June 21 I wrote:

In Serra Nova, the "sharks" are getting worried and are stepping up their plans. The Bordon *fazenda* has decided to "clear" the forest up to the edge of their "cut," so that, from now on, all hopes of a *posseiro* takeover will be nipped in the bud.... We have decided to step up the date of the missionary campaign for Serra Nova.

And, on July 20:

I am in Brasilia, which is always so light and open. I just came from the SNI (National Information Service).

Yesterday I was at INCRA (National Institute for Colonization and Agrarian Reform). I came here to do something about the Serra Nova problem.

7

We had begun to bring our anguished powerlessness to the attention of some of the surrounding sectors of the church in Brazil. We were beginning to see that this problem was not ours alone, and that we alone could not solve it. We felt that, at the very least, "the" church of the country should make some pronouncement on this issue, if it wished to be faithful to the needs of the hour and to its own mission.

5/7/71: In Goiânia I visited Dom Fernando (archbishop of that city and president of the West Central Region of the NCCB) and told him of my concerns: Transamazon, latifundios, deportation, haphazard pastoral care for the human groups affected. . . . He accepted my suggestions: to petition the national headquarters of the Council of Bishops to sponsor a study on the latifundio in this country, and a meeting of bishops and vicars in the area affected by Amazonian phenomenon. Was it to be simply "Amazonia for the Amazonians," or was it to be for all the migrants—northeasterners, Goianians, Mato Grossans—all those who were going to populate (by force? seduced by publicity campaigns and politicans' promises?) the newly explored territories?

The seminar in Rio (on the pastoral needs and care of Amazonia), on the 14th, 15th and 16th, was a good exposition of the socio-political problems of Amazonia. It now remained for the Representative Commission of the NCCB, which was to meet in August, to spell out its meaning in concrete and effective detail.

During the seminar I insisted on the danger of setting a higher value on the Transamazon than on Amazonia itself. We all know that there is a certain amount of fear on the part of the "official" church, whenever crucial social problems present themselves. There is a great deal of "politics" that is called prudence. Sometimes it is sincere; sometimes naive; sometimes, cowardly and outright compromising. . . .

On May 18 I noted:

Sunday, we (all the inhabitants of Pontinópolis, and dozens of families who had traveled from many leagues away, men, women, and children) waited in vain for the arrival of Senhor Ariosto here in Pontinópolis. Once again he had broken his word. We were prepared to receive him, and with arguments drawn from the law itself. In my irritation, I told the people: "Not even God keeps anyone waiting like this!"

This show of solidarity with the people in their anger won me the out and out confidence of the local leadership (after two whole years, during which I had had only the barest apparent show of confidence!).

That same day, I copied down this bit of advice from Confucius:

If you want to win for a day, give food. If you want to win for a year, plant grain. If you want to win forever, instruct the people.

On June 24, I unburdened myself of the following statement:

Ratifying injustice is an all too "Catholic" sin. In this, the church has been guilty for many centuries now. She ought to admit it, deplore it, and become converted.

8

Meanwhile, the news that I had been nominated bishop had arrived from the Vatican. I had already written my letter declining the appointment, and was about to mail it, when Dom Tomás Balduino, the friendly bishop of Goiás, happened to pass through São Félix. Dom Tomás was the pilot of a little red and white airplane, which always seemed to appear in our skies like a providential bird. He strongly urged me not to send the letter, and to wait until we could all talk it over on the occasion of Manuel's ordination on August 7.

It's three years since Manuel and I arrived in São Félix. Three years, as long as three decades and as hard as three novitiates. Three years, as good as three Masses . . . (So I commented in my diary for July 30th).

On Saturday, August 7, 1971, Manuel Luzón, my "companion of the first hour," always as good and faithful as a tree of noble wood, was ordained a priest of Christ for his people of this Mato Grosso, thus fulfilling a dream that he had cultivated through long years of humble service.

On Sunday, the 8th, all the local Padres and Sisters got together with Dom Tomás, since the word was now out

about my nomination. They discussed the pros and cons of my case and accepted me as their future bishop. I suppose they decided that a known evil was easier to deal with than an unknown good. Then Dom Tomás called me in. I accepted without any illusions (they were long gone, anyhow). Once more I reminded them all of my limitations and idiosyncrasies (my "charisma," perhaps). And I reaffirmed my irrevocable decision to follow the people of Serra Nova—or any other persecuted town in my vicariate—into exile, if they were ever deported. And I would not let my episcopal office stand in the way....
Life went on.

Next Saturday I went out with some thirty men (from Serra Nova), to take down some trees for a "clearing" that was being opened in the dense thicket about five kilometers away. (Even Benedito *"Boca-Quente"*— "Hot-Mouth," who was in league with the *fazendas,* had to admire the job: "One helluva clearing!") It was a marvelous day of *mutirao*—"community work." A young lad and I acted as waterboys for the axe-swinging workers. This was one day when I actually enjoyed seeing trees felled: plunging, like olympic divers, into the momentarily parted waters of a whole people that had come together in a living stream. They were opening up a great door, to let in the sun and the future, and the flying leaves of the shaken trees danced in the air like confetti at the festival of freedom....

But within me some warning sounded. Anxiety was back, full circle. Hope sometimes seems to curdle within us. Faith is being put to the test, and I want to "know" the One I have put my trust in....

It was on this "clearing" day that I wrote—on a banana-leaf, using the tip of my jack-knife as a pen—the "Hymn of Serra Nova," which has been sung so often in many rural areas of Brazil, that its name has been changed to the "Hymn of the Rural Community":

> We are a people's people,
> we are the People of God.
> We want a land on this earth;
> we've already a land in heaven. . . .

On the same page of my diary for August 16, I went on:

I feel a need to confess; perhaps, to purify myself, in every way. I am going to be consecrated bishop. On the 23rd of October! Without consciously planning it (even trying to fight it off), it will be the feastday of St. Anthony Mary Claret. I am happy, because things turned out so providentially to make it happen on that day.

I am calling out to the Virgin, in a sort of instinctive need for faith and poverty. Our Lady of the Squatters! Powerful and good as you are, attend to the hopes of this inheritance! Holy Mother of the apostles of Jesus, make me a bishop in accordance with the Spirit of your Son.

AUGUST 17:

I have decided not to wear ring, mitre, or crozier. Yesterday I sketched out an invitation that would explain why I have decided on this style of dress; I think it is a matter of simple logic. I'm not doing it as a lesson to anybody. I'm doing it as a duty, in order to be consistent with who I am.

The cover of the invitation bears a reproduction of a shepherd's horn and lasso, taken from the illustrations drawn by the northeastern artist, Poty. The text reads as follows:

> Your *mitre* will be: the straw hat of a *sertanejo;* sunlight and moonlight; rainy and clear weather; the glance of the poor with whom you walk and the glorious glance of Christ, the Lord.
>
> Your *crozier* will be: the gospel truth and the trust of your people in you.
>
> Your *ring* will be: fidelity to the new covenant of the God who frees and fidelity to the people of this land.
>
> You shall have no other *shield* than the power of hope and freedom of the Children of God.
>
> You shall wear no other *gloves* than the service of love.

Tensions were mounting at Serra Nova. The Bordon Company was threatening to kill me and Moura (the boy who accompanied me on my missionary campaigns), and to burn the town to the ground. Lulú—a friendly *posseiro* who had been imprisoned twice and tortured by the latifundio and the forces of repression—was to be ambushed in the forest by the *fazenda's* contractor, Benedito Boca-Quente. "Boca quente" means "hot mouth" and refers to the smoking mouth of his gun-barrel. And they had put a price on my life, time and time again, during the whole month of October, so as to prevent, if they could, my episcopal consecration. They were offering, for my head, as anyone can read in the confession signed by the would-be assassin, in the presence of the federal police: "a thousand *cruzeiros,* a 38 revolver, and a ticket of freedom that could be used at will."

AUGUST 25:

It is really wearying, this struggle for the land, because one is surrounded on all sides by a wall of fire. . . .

Hope—that "land beyond encroachments"—the stability of the *patrimonio,* the life of this whole prelature, the future and eternal peace of everyone: all these things are as hard to bear as martyrdom. Hoping is dying enough! Sometimes I feel the night closing in on me and I feel a numb hankering just to rest. At the same time I feel the call of destiny (the supreme destiny of the Love that has trusted in me!), to keep on going, despite the fight within me, the night within me, the death within me. But also, and definitively: the Christ within me!

AUGUST 26:

"Hope never fails," says Paul in today's reading from the breviary.

I shall never be able to doubt the radical evil of the oppressive structures (of capitalism). I shall never be able to doubt the legitimacy of the oppressed classes' struggle to be free. No oppressive government is going to free the oppressed! I also believe more firmly every day, that it is necessary to demythologize private property.

I am reading González Ruiz' book: *Evangelical Poverty and the Advancement of Peoples.* A book filled with luminous, exciting hints.

Evangelizing means promoting the advancement of people, with the added "more" of the free gift of Christ. Only the evangelizer promotes the advancement of man to his ultimate goal. But how difficult it will be for him who would evangelize, without at the same time promoting human advancement!

For some days now, I have been renewing my total self-offering. Every day poorer and more dispossessed. Sometimes I feel that there's nothing left of me but weakness—physical and moral—nothing but frayed nerves and a "fatal" hope....

SEPTEMBER 18:

So I'm going to be a bishop. Is it just something simple, like that, or is it something mysterious or inevitable? For sure, it's something Christian. That's how things work in the church.... I have written to the monasteries of La Oliva and El Goloso, and to many other communities and friends, asking for prayer. It comforts me to know that we have these "bases" in the vanguard of the rear guard—or rather, in the vanguard of the vanguard, to put it more exactly.

SEPTEMBER 24:

Cardinal Marty says: The bishop is the man of faith for his people. He is the father who teaches a community how to articulate, to profess and speak out its faith. And to live it: for it is only the witness of a church that is evangelizing. That is why the first mission of a bishop is to be a prophet.... The prophet is one who tells the truth, in the presence of the whole people.

It was October already. I was extremely busy drawing up a pastoral letter: *An Amazonian Church's Struggle against Landed Estates and against Social Marginalization,* which I was going to launch on the occasion of my episcopal consecration. In my diary for October 12, I wrote:

I know that this is going to arouse opposition, but I think that it's my duty to write it. It hasn't been easy. And it's a risk in itself, almost a total challenge.

At the beginning of September, the *fazendeiros,* with the blessings of the man we'll just call "the good Father X," attempted to block my episcopal consecration: first, with my Claretian superiors in São Paulo; then, in Rio, with the Apostolic Nuncio. During those days the clan of the powerful spread out on the local level, going from town to town, planting the seeds of the great defamation: we were all communists, subversives, foreigners....

OCTOBER 19:

I feel within me a great ideological, ascetical, and emotional tension, between meekness and anger. Both of them—at the right time and in the right dosage—are evangelical. This *sertao* leaves its scars and wounds. I hope that death will transform into love—by some retrospective power—all of my poor life.

From several quarters I have received the message: Beware of becoming a prophet out of vainglory. Beware of favoring only one side. Beware (as someone said) of getting involved in class-struggle. I hope, rather, that the very Spirit of Jesus will be "ware" of me. I am going to try to be faithful with a remorseful humility and with a daily and realistic liberty. My vocation—as a man, as a Christian, as a bishop—is one of "not letting myself be mistaken. . . ."

OCTOBER 30:

I am a bishop. Since the 23rd. My episcopal consecration was carried out in the greatest simplicity and, inevitably, in a spirit of utter realism, commitment, and self-surrender.

Many friends accompanied me. And the Spirit of Jesus was very present.

No grand emotions. No fearful responsibilities. It was like a new confirmation. Like the ultimate demand.

I am an apostle, a bishop of the church of Jesus. I must trust in the Spirit of the Risen Lord which gives life to his church. I must serve the People of God with full liberty and dedication.

The ordination took place on the banks of the Araguaia, at nightfall. A *sertanejo* straw hat, a *remo-borduna* walking stick carved out of Brazil wood (with images of a road, a hunt, and a fishing catch) by the Tapirapé Indians: these were my episcopal emblems—the mitre and crozier of that dignity which would have to be one of service. The ring, a copy of the one that Paul VI gave to all the bishops at Vatican II (sent to me as a surprise gift from friends in Spain), I sent back to Spain, as an act of filial homage to my mother. During the homily, I stated once more—but more publicly and definitively—my option for the poor and the oppressed.

10

My pastoral denunciation, *An Amazonian Church* ... (consisting of 123 pages crammed with documentation that has never been rebutted), appeared as planned, on the day of my episcopal ordination. It appeared, naturally, without the name of the printer and, just as naturally, it was banned by General Canepa, national director of the federal police. In the following preliminary note, I gave my justification for publishing the document:

After three years of "mission" in the north of Mato Grosso, together with other priests, religious, and laypersons, I have striven in word, in silence, in suffering, and in the life of the people, to discern the signs of the time and the place. Now, on the occasion of my episcopal consecration, I feel the need and the duty to share publicly, on a nation-wide level, with the church and with conscientious people everywhere, the anguishing and urgent situation I have discovered.

I am doing this in order to make this church known to its sister churches, and to the church. I am doing it to seek and to promote—again, within the framework of the church—a deeper communion, a truer collegiality, and a more committed corresponsibility. Perhaps, too, to awaken and evoke individual responses and vocations. . . .

No church can live in isolation. Every church is universal, in the communion of one and the same hope, and in the common service of the love of Christ, who liberates and saves us. ... "Each part contributes through its own special gifts to the well being of the other parts and to that of the whole church, so that the whole and each of its parts grow through mutual sharing and common effort to attain fullness in unity" (*Lumen Gentium*, 13).

The publicity which the ongoing projects and accomplishments in Amazonia have received, as well as the priority they have been given by the Brazilian church through its National Council of Bishops, provide new reasons that justify my public declaration.

If it is true that "the first mission of a bishop is to be a prophet," and that "the prophet is one who speaks the truth in the presence of the whole people," and that "to be a bishop is to be the voice of those who have no voice" (Cardinal Marty), then I could not—honestly—stand by silently, when I had received the fullness of priestly service.

Reactions were immediate, both at home and abroad. *O Estado de São Paul*—capitalist, liberal, conservative—dedicated a three-column, full-page editorial to "the bad faith and demagoguery of this bishop," indicting me as a "raving prelate," "undocumented," "man of bad faith," "pharisaical demagogue," "provocateur of the government," and as having "an intelligence as lacking in acumen as it is in scruples." *O Jornal do Brasil,* however, called attention to the sweeping character of the denunciation and the urgency of checking it out. The Brazilian press in general, influenced as it is by the government, attacked me. The foreign press stressed the timeliness and significance of a voice from the church which uncovered a vast and as yet relatively unmined vein for public opinion. The presidency of the National Council of Bishops approved

my document, and many bishops, Christian communities,
as well as groups and individuals committed to social
causes—both in Brazil and abroad—manifested their solidarity with me.

I believe that my "pastoral" was a consciousness-raising
moment of truth for many people. And a point of departure.

On November 5, I wrote in my diary:

> São Félix continues tense. For various reasons. Cer-
> tain reactions against the document. Accusations against
> the Padres. Quarrels. Deaths... and a visit from the
> federal police that was peculiarly significant, especially
> since they were asking all sorts of questions about the
> doings of the Padres and the professors....

Benedito Boca-Quente finally left the *fazenda,* after asking five people to kill him. Thank God no one had enough
homicidal "courage" to oblige him. Later we learned that
he had met his end in Goiás, and I have prayed many times
for this—desperate—companion and wayfarer.

On November 10, the town of Serra Nova went to work
with wirecutters and broke through the fence of the Bordon *fazenda* that was strangling them. The 12th saw the
arrival of Captains Moacir and João Evangelista, with
whom we are, unfortunately, well-acquainted. They began
a circle of investigations, police and military interventions,
looting, imprisonments ... against the pastoral team of the
prelature and against the defenseless people of the region.

In January of 1972 I had gone to Brasilia to attempt an
impossible dialogue with the higher authorities, concerning the problems of Santa Terezinha and Father Jentel

with the Codeara Company, and the overall land-problem in our vicinity.

On the 20th I wrote in my diary:

This morning Dom Ivo (the Secretary General of the Council of Bishops) and I had a long interview with the Minister of Justice, Alfredo Buzaid. In short, the minister asked me for a truce of silence. Meanwhile, he—as main go-between in the dialogue between the government and the "official" church?—would get in touch with the ministers involved in the matters of our prelature (i.e., of the interior, of agriculture, and of public works) and even with the president of the republic. He said that he would also enter into dialogues (accusations, actually) with the Codeara, Bordon, and Frenova Companies. Then we would meet again, after (Buzaid stressed the "after") Carnival.

He asked us not to forget that the government was made up of (and I quote), "Catholics, non-Catholics, anti-Catholics, and Masons." He said that he was deeply moved at all injustice. He did not accept my blanket condemnation of the latifundio and, in a somewhat nuanced form, he defended the official state position: Progress must come, and someone will have to be sacrificed in the process. The fewest possible and to the least degree possible, he added, very timidly. . . . The only latifundio that he would quarrel with was one that was not producing. I told him that in that case, I would condemn minifundios as well as latifundios. But my main point, I hammered home to him, was the needs of particular men, particular families, without land, without rights, and without a future. . . . We accepted the truce. We will pray. We will open our eyes and our hearts. We will await the passing of Carnival. Afterward comes Lent, the Passion, Easter.

In Brasilia, some people who work at INCRA told Father Francisco an amusing story. It seems that Dr. Seixas, one of the owners of Codeara and vice-president of the Agro-cattle Association of Amazonia, has just asked INCRA for their support in instituting proceedings against me on the basis of insanity. . . .

In São Félix, at the beginning of February, we had a crash-course in overall review and planning for the prelature, led by the famous teacher and our very good friend, María Nilde Mascellani, who had often been tried and imprisoned in our common cause of justice. Priestly and lay reinforcements had arrived in our vicariate. We were organizing our work for the coming year.

During this short course in planning, we drew up the following list of "Constant Problems Encountered in the Prelature":

1. Conflict between *latifundias* and *posseiros*.
2. Lack of basic health care.
3. Unjust laboring conditions affecting all classes of employees: bargemen, peons, professors.
4. Isolation of all sorts: roads, mail, climate (the rains).
5. Faulty education: illiteracy, semiilliteracy, poorly prepared teachers, lack of equipment, buildings, etc., formal education inadequate to cope with the real problems of the region.

6. Monopolistic political interference (a system of deals between politicians, landholders, merchants, and others).
7. Plight of the peons as a transient population, subjected to a system of enslavement and isolation.
8. Survival of the Indians as an ethnic group.
9. Business monopolies.
10. *Retirantismo* (policy of perpetual migrancy).
11. High incidence of irregular family life and prostitution.
12. Spirit of passivity and fatalism.
13. Total lack of leisure time.
14. Lowest degree of self-sustaining agriculture.
15. Predominance of odd beliefs and superstitions (religiosity vs. faith).
16. Behavioral patterns established in the community: revenge, violence, boasting, drunkenness, indolence, prostitution.
17. Lack of a work market: work stoppages and underemployment.
18. Cultural peculiarities (local languages, etc.).
19. Lack of any real substructure for stimulating cultural or pastoral growth.
20. Present government policies continually threatening the survival and the future of the people of the region.
21. Working groups of outsiders, and their acculturation.

Starting from our analysis of these problems, we set about logically establishing overall priorities, formulating programs and spelling out our general objective of "developing a permanent process of struggle for the libera-

tion of man and for the establishment of just relationships," within the framework and means of the local
church.

The new meeting between Dom Ivo, myself, and Minister Buzaid kept being postponed. Meanwhile, in Goiânia,
someone hit on the idea of forming a "nongroup" of un-
pretentious, plain-speaking bishops, committed to the
same pastoral objectives. From this "nongroup," some of
the most significant initiatives, documents, attitudes, and
interventions for the Brazilian church have been issued
during the past three years.

11

The Codeara Company, after six years of aggressive and
impertinent actions against the *posseiros* of the region, finally turned their tractors against the new walk-in clinic
being built at Santa Terezinha. Father Jentel came to see
me in Goiânia, to tell me of this latest affront, and to ask
my opinion on what course we should take.

I roundly ruled out any more fruitless appeals to the
authorities. We had laid our claim before the district
judge; that was enough (besides, it was useless). Father
Francisco, who set great store by the law, felt outraged. I
left the choice up to him. My decision, in any case, was
irrevocable. Finally, he agreed with me, and went back to
Santa Terezinha to start work on the clinic all over
again. . . .

Around this time an "official" theologian of the Council
of Bishops informed a group of the regional secretaries of
the Council in Rio, that I was going to get into a "mess"
with the Holy See over some of the expressions I used in
my pastoral; and also, he added, because "it was well

known that the pastoral had been written by a bunch of leftists from São Paulo."

The bitterness and the tension were mounting.

3/19/72: Feast of St. Joseph. Brasilia. The "other" Brasilia of rectangular buildings, waiting-rooms, audiences, lies. I have been here two weeks.

On the evening of the 3rd, provoked by a new attempt at invasion and destruction, a group of *posseiros* defended the clinic at Santa Terezinha—and their own freedom—with shots. . . . Eight of the *"jagunços"* (bullies) from Codeara were wounded. And for fifteen days there has been a running exchange of "you-tell-me's-and-I'll-tell-you's" in the press, in various ministries and in trips. The repression on the part of those in power (economic, political, police, and military power) has been downright cynical. Five innocent men from Santa Terezinha have been imprisoned in Cuiabá, and thirty or forty *posseiros* have slipped into the forests. . . .

Fifteen days of real Lent, spent between anger and prayer, in the Passion of the People, beneath the hard and shining hope of Jesus, the liberator.

I have learned a lot about politics and the church.

The present government of Brazil is a Nazi terrorist scheme. The economic powers impose the law and put a muzzle on justice.

3/21: Still in Brasilia! Last night the heads of the Council of Bishops arrived. They have come here mainly on account of the business at Santa Terezinha. They are concerned and they are inclined to think that, as Dom

Aloisio sadly put it, this may drag on forever, within the means at our disposal.

Friday I had an outspoken interview with Buzaid. His nauseating cynicism upset me so, that I refused the coffee he offered me, just as I refused to accept any more of his delays and mendacious mediations. Sunday he phoned the governor of Cuiabá, José Fragelli. The latter said, quite aggressively: "I will not release my grip." He added that he considered the *posseiros* of Santa Terezinha "as common criminals," and promised that "if Padre Jentel ever shows up here (in Cuiabá, the state capitol of Mato Grosso), I will issue an order for his arrest, because he is the mastermind behind this crime." My response to this was that I myself, and not Padre Francisco, was the "mastermind," and that I assumed and still assume full responsibility for what happened at Santa Terezinha, both as regards the mission and as regards the *posseiros*. . . .

April 6: I spent some days in Santa Terezinha. And I visited the *posseiros* hidden in the *mata*. And, almost symbolically, I harvested rice.

It was while I was doing this that the following poem came to me:

> *Song of the Sickle and the Sheaf**
> With a callus for a ring
> the bishop was chopping rice.
> Bishop "Hammer
> and Sickle"?

*A merely literal translation, without the rime or resonance of the original.

They will call me subversive
and I'll tell them: I am.
For my struggling people I live.
With my marching people I go.

I have a guerrilla's faith
and a love of revolution.
And between gospel and song
I suffer and say what I will.
If I scandalize, well, first
I burnt my own heart
in the fire of this Passion,
on the cross of his same wood.

I incite to subversion
against power and money.
I want to subvert a Law
that perverts the people into a herd
and the government into a butcher.
(My shepherd became a lamb.
My king became a servant.)

I believe in the International
of heads held high,
of voices speaking equal to equal
and of hands intertwined . . .
I call "order" an evil
and "progress" a lie.
I have less peace than wrath.
I have more love than peace.

. . . I believe in the sickle and the sheaf
of these fallen heads of grain:

one death and so many lives!
I believe in this sickle advancing
—beneath this sun without mask
and in a common hope—
how curved it is, and tenacious!

The Codeara Company—basking complacently in the
shade of the police state—continues with its irritations.
Fifteen days ago they raised a control gate and stretched
a chain across the public roadway that leads to the *roças*
(clearings) of the *posseiros.* There they ask the name of
anyone who wants to pass. And they wouldn't let the car
we were driving in pass. A little Berlin Wall in the forest:
"*O colchete da vergonha* . . . the shameful clasp."

Canuto and I concelebrated Holy Thursday in Santa
Terezinha. (Fr. Antonio Canuto had taken the place of Fr.
Jentel, who had to leave Santa Terezinha on the night of
the 3rd, since he had aided me in our recourse to the
Council of Bishops and the press, in Brasilia and Rio.) The
Sisters were there, too. It was a very real eucharist.

Five citizens of Santa Terezinha are imprisoned in
Cuiabá, held there as hostages to the fury of the latifundio,
by the governor and the police. And more than thirty men
are hiding in the ricefields and forests. Up to their knees in
water, and in that climate of persecution. Images of a
homefront Vietnam violently break out in my brain.

Pedrito is in Goiânia, in Brasilia. So is Fr. Francisco.
Sister María de Lourdes, who was sent to Cuiabá to find
out about the prisoners, has not returned yet. And we have
to come to a quick decision on the lot of the *posseiros* hiding
in the *mata.*

Yesterday Terezinha and Tadeu arrived by plane, together with Maroto's woman. (Maroto was one of the five imprisoned.) The woman had to be operated on immediately—a Caesarean section—and gave birth to a girl. The child was born with a defect in her mouth. But she is alive and will get better. This is the fourth flower of freedom for Santa Terezinha.

In those days I used to say that March 3, the day of the defense of the clinic, should be celebrated as a sort of "*sertão* independence day." It was like our little "Prague springtime"—a date of paschal liberation.

Letters of support were coming in. And hope kept on, victorious over human anguish and despair. There were misunderstandings and rebuffs as well. Our official notice from the heads of the Council of Bishops, for example. (The notice which the Council published was somewhat ambiguous, because of its extremely "prudent language," which was the result of the different points of view of its authors, and this left us with a certain lack of official backing.)

That same April 6, I added:

"One must harden oneself, yet never lose tenderness," as Che used to say. The Lord said that one must fight without hatred, love one's enemy, make war in peace. Anger, even weapons, blood, the repressions and aggressions of these days: all call me to a greater understanding, to a charity-in-spite-of-all and, in the long run, to the peace of Christ. Perhaps the limit we've arrived at—like all limits—may turn out to have been a good, spontaneous lesson. This in no way means retreating, let alone compromising. "I have come not to bring peace but a sword." "My peace I leave you . . . not as the world gives it." "The peace of our Passover."

4/8: We have to make a decision about the five in jail in Cuiabá and about the *posseiros* hidden in the forest. This morning I awoke very early, with a start, at the thought of the situation of these men of our people. Freedom costs dearly! As I read in some review the other day: "The more the forces of money and oligarchy are shaken, the more clearly one perceives their overpowering talent for enslavement."

4/14: I've been in Santa Terezinha for a week, chopping rice, walking through roads, *mata,* and rice paddies. We have met with the *posseiros* in hiding and with their families. Last night and early this morning, I said Mass in Tapirapé. After several days of not being able to say Mass, I was hungry for eucharist.

Altair (a lay team-member who worked in Porto Alegre, almost at the headwaters of the Tapirapé River, and also in Santa Terezinha) is imprisoned in the miserable little hole of the local jail. He's been there seven days, now.... The Codeara Company persists in its campaign of nuisances: they've closed both exits from the town. We have had no details from Brasilia. Father Francisco is still there. Nothing will come of it all anyway, unless it comes from the unity and hardheadedness of the people. There is no force to equal the desperate hope of the poor!

The "Church of the *Mata*" has been born. God keep it in the hollow of his hand!

4/17: Yesterday was "*domingo do doce*" (sweets Sunday), and we had kettlesfull of papaya and calabash candy with the women and children of the *posseiros*. Then Mass at the "Antonio Grosso." Mass again at the *roça grande* (the great clearing), with the men in hiding. The altar was a burnt tree-stump, with a shotgun leaning against it, draped in a *posseiro's surroncico*. Evening was falling, and the gospel told the story of the two men walking along the road to Emmaus. The persecuted men attending the Mass—rather hungry, rather anxious, suffering greatly—listened to the reading, enthralled by it.

Sister Beatrice gave them a tetanus vaccination. Then, as we began to relax, we all laughed a little.

Twilight cast a thick, amber light on the premonitory clouds that were piling up behind the tall, dense forest.

Today, Psalm 84 tells us "Happy are they whose strength you are! Their hearts are set upon pilgrimage. When they cross the parched valley, they shall turn it into a spring." Then James tells us: "Speak and act as men destined to be judged under the law of liberty."

4/27: Feast of *la Verge de Montserrat*. I remembered my mother at Mass, asking that she be given "la llibertad d'esperit, la força de l'Esperança, el sentit de la comunió i de la corresponsabilitat eclesial . . ." (freedom of spirit, the power of hope, the feeling of communion and of ecclesial corresponsibility). Whenever I mention family or home, my diary lapses into Catalán.

There is a decree of expulsion hanging over Fr. Francisco's head. I have gone to the National Information Service, the federal police, the Franch Embassy, the nunciature, etc. But diplomacy ill-accords with the gospel, and politics is not given either to speaking the truth or to serving justice.

4/28: I'm still in Goiânia. With a fever. Another young helper of mine, Pontin, is down with his first attack of malaria, in the Hospital das Clínicas. . . .

Now it was May. I returned to Santa Terezinha and then went on by plane to Porto Alegre, near the source of the Tapirapé. The president of INCRA and his wife had visited Santa Terezinha *incognito*. The result was a solution, in principle, of the basic land-problem. Each *posseiro* was to receive 100 hectares of land, as stipulated for this region by presidential decree of April 7, which came about precisely because of the conflict between Santa Terezinha and Codeara. (But, as I write these lines, it is still not clear just how all the *posseiros* are actually going to *get* these rights.) In any case, the problems of the "criminals in the forest" and of the planned deportation of Francisco, were in other hands: the arbitrary, almighty, steel grip of the Department of National Security. The "inquest into the expulsion" of Fr. Jentel, which he and I were following very closely (rebutting its accusations, trying to stir up some public interest in the case, ridiculing the "official" version of the proceedings), was becoming a real farce.

On May 19 I wrote:

Altair is still in jail, this time in Cuiabá. Rosa and Chico are safe, although they are by now far, far away.

Rosa and Chico were a young married couple who worked at Santa Terezinha, but had had to flee—in good time, thank God!—both from the mission and from Brazil. And they are still fleeing, suffering, among other things, the lot of exiles, and generously serving the cause of the oppressed wherever they go.

Our little church is suffering persecution for the sake of the gospel of justice, which is beyond a shadow of a doubt the gospel of Jesus.

6/3: I am in Santa Terezinha again, beginning once more to live a life at the mercy of the whims of others. Dom Tomás, Francisco, and I traveled to Santarém in his little "put-put" of an airplane. It was a surprise-filled journey over Amazonia: clouds and virgin forest. Then came the discovery of the Xingu and, past Santarém, the confluence of the Tapajós and the mighty Amazon, where they merge to form what seems a lordly stretch of sea. On the way back—during a few hours of the night and early morning—I gained a nodding acquaintance with Belém and its great estuary.

We were lost for a while, somewhere between Marabá and Altamira, crossing that endless tract of dense forest. The rain was blinding, our pilot (Dom Tomás) was sweating, and all three of us were feeling a bit queasy at the uneven ratio between our flimsy craft above, and the abyss of clouds and forest below.

Pará, in its human types, is markedly aboriginal. This is one place, at least, where the Indians didn't die off.

We were in Santarém seven days for a pastoral meeting of the representatives of Northern Regions I and II of the National Council of Bishops (plus a few representatives from the rest of legal Amazonia). It was a good meeting, despite its somewhat limited outlook and its procedural fits and starts. It was an excellent opportunity, all in all, to get a closeup view both of Amazonia's natural resources and its hierarchy.

(During this pastoral meeting at Santarém, we heard a radio broadcast by the minister of justice, Buzaid, announcing the expulsion of Fr. Jentel. So, it was already a *fait accompli*! But it would still have to face the scrutiny of public opinion, especially in the foreign press.)

... When we arrived back in Santa Terezinha, the

inevitable Codeara and their bought-off police were waiting for us. They were in hopes of catching Fr. Francisco, so they stopped Dom Tomás' plane. We had to get out, answer their questions and somehow control our rising irritation, with mixed feelings of passion and peace. . . .

While Dom Tomás managed to get out to say Mass for the Little Sisters of Charles de Foucauld in the village of Tapirapé, Canuto and I celebrated at "el morro" (on the hill overlooking Santa Terezinha where, thirty years earlier, the Dominicans of the vicariate of Conceição do Araguaia had built the solid and sober "parish" church, in honor of Therese, the "missionary" saint of Lisieux). There was a good crowd present. The air was clear and tense with joy. The Liturgy of the Word was from the tenth chapter of Matthew: "Behold, I am sending you out like sheep among wolves. . . . Do not be afraid. . . . Whoever acknowledges me before men. . . ."

6/9: Feast of the Sacred Heart of Jesus. Whether the title is outdated or not (because of the sentimental piety attached to it in the past), the truth it stands for is really eternal: God's love in Christ Jesus, "the man who, out of love for the Father, is *the* man for others."

I went to Campo Grande, the economic capital of Mato Grosso and the seat of the military tribunal, where the future of the forty "forest criminals" was being thrashed out, and where Fr. Jentel would eventually be tried and sentenced.

6/17: I have spoken with the presiding judge and with the lawyer appointed for Francisco's defense. The trial has been postponed until July 3. It seems that they were waiting here to take Francisco by surprise. (They were also trying to take him by surprise in São Félix, Santa Trezinha, Goiânia, Brasilia, Rio and São Paulo. In all these places, the police were hot on his tracks that very day.) Colonel Ivo de Albuquerque, the state secretary of security, is furious and would like to devour "those Padres from São Félix." He has an acute case of "security-itis," so we must both excuse him and evade him.

6/22: Barra do Garças: dust, managers, banks, warehouses—and an allergy for that nitpicking clutch of local politicos. I passed through Rondonópolis and Cuiabá. We visited with Dom Osorio, the very obliging bishop of Rondonópolis. Then I went to see the retired general who is the new secretary of public security for the state of Mato Grosso. I also visited Dr. Saavedra, of INCRA. Clearly, all these visits got me exactly nowhere. By no means would the *fazendas* be disappropriated. The neocapitalist philosophy of the present régime will prevail. The poor will be cared for with benevolent crumbs and leftovers of an alms.

This last week there was a practice "alert" for the military in Santa Terezinha. "Alert" is a word inherited from the old general of public security.

Tomorrow morning I'll leave for São Félix. The minibus that was bringing us from Cuiabá broke down, and there we were, stuck in a ditch, from four in the morning until two-something in the afternoon. This made me miss the next bus for São Félix.

One geographic-sentimental encounter lingers in my memory. En route from Rondoópolis to Cuiabá, I passed through the Chapadão de São Vicente, the source of our Rio das Mortes. And in Cuiabá—still in its first, naive flush of city-building—I discovered one of the few remaining monuments of the colonial era. The Jesuit Church of the Holy Rosary, white and rose-maroon, simple and free of external ornament, stands as a pretty tribute to a past that was, perhaps, not so pretty.

. . . Paul VI, in his message to the church on the eve of the World Day of Prayer for Vocations, defines the vocation to the priesthood as follows: "A commitment which demands availability, an interior attitude and a risk, a willingness to break with any future project that proceeds from merely human hope."

On July 1, Eugenio Consoli was ordained: the second priest ordained in the prelature and the first to be ordained by me. I had earlier informed the people about the forthcoming event, in a sort of *sertanejo* pastoral letter.

The ordination took place in the straw hut of Silvano, a *posseiro*. The hut is just off the road that leads from São Félix to Barra do Garças, thus winning Eugenio the future nickname of "*o Padre da Estrada*" (the street Padre). That was the most euphorically communitarian liturgy our church ever celebrated. People came from miles around, on foot and on horseback. It was a motley crowd. We talked, prayed, and sang spontaneously. Lulú hung a string of beans on the burnt-wood cross that presided over the gathering, "because," he explained, "the *sertanejo* knows what it costs to harvest a few beans. . . ." Eugenio, his family, his friends, I and the people, all took turns speaking out what we felt the event meant to each one of us, and why we were glad to have Eugenio as a priest just then and there.

12

Still July:

7/18: Here in the hot, breezy, bright-blue patio of our house at São Félix, I have just finished reading the autobiographic volume which José María González-Ruiz wrote for the series, "The Credo that has Given Meaning to My Life," A pilgrimage of rebellious fidelity, biblically lucid, humanly realistic and consistent with the demands of everyday life, a book which is both aware of, and in step with, history. Here is a Christian—head and heart—this admirable González-Ruiz: "Although God is gratuitous, he's not superfluous. . . . God is at the base of it all. . . . To believe is to commit oneself. . . ." If a person's starting point is the gratuitousness of hope, he can simply and joyously thumb his nose at every ideology, every pessimism, every oppression, every future. . . .

I've just got some new glasses. I'm getting more near-sighted all the time. (Now I have cataracts, too. The one in my left eye is pretty well advanced, and will have to be operated on sometime this year.) Well, that's the wear and tear of life for you! I'll just have to look more carefully and remember what I've already seen. And listen, too—"seeing" with my ears!

At certain heights in life, hope seems to fill the air with the slow, sweet smell of bread baking in the oven.

7/21: Last night, at the Tapirapé village, we celebrated a deeply-shared Mass. Sisters Abigail and Genevieve, together with Eugenio, Pontin, Jean Loup, Matos, and me, were there. Afterwards, at a gathering that was half-*Aruana,* half-soíree, we sat beneath the crescent moon and had a wonderful conversation.

The new projects of FUNAI are creating a climate of tension in the village. FUNAI wants to build God knows how many houses and a "banana-candy factory" (whatever that might be!). Do they want to rob the village of its whole "mission" character? The Little Sisters have remarked that the chief at the post "prescinds" from them.... The Indians even speak of threats from the police.... One of the owners of the Tapiraguaia *fazenda* adjoining Tapirapé, went there yesterday to visit the *roça,* and mentioned that several boundary surveys are being plotted in Brasilia.

8/5: Traveling along the highway from Barra, I could sense how widely and quickly the *fazendas* are spreading: enveloping all, invading all. I was told that the *fazendeiro* Halim (?), from Anápolis, was cutting into the land of the Xavante Indians of Porto Pimentel, just two kilometers from their village....

I have started reading Ernesto Cardenal's *Homage to the American Indians.* Its message is prophetic and of worldwide dimensions: a lively piece of historical writing and an indictment.

My eyes hurt. And I feel run-down—all the time—with the accumulated weight of bitterness, preoccupations, interferences....

8/12: I have spent three days in the village of Tapirapé. With the Little Sisters, and with Moura and Ilda, who are preparing the "first grade" of the Tapirapé Indians. Luis and Eunice (who is soon due to deliver her baby) will be the "professors" for 1973.

... Colonel Clovis of INCRA, and two land-surveyors, were here in the village with Canuto, looking for me. I was twenty-two kilometers away, in the *roça.* The colonel—and the ever-ambiguous Dr. Peixoto—are "quite upset." We can't agree on the boundaries they've set for the *posseiros* of Santa Terezinha, since they will do nothing to solve the town's problems.

8/17: A peon who just slept off his last drinking spree has finally managed to get some tea down. His liver hurts. The poor devil tells me: "It's been three months since I had a drink." This morning a group met me on the street, near the cemetery. They were looking for some of their buddies. They told me the same old story we keep hearing lately: 200 peons from Piauí were brought here under false pretenses by the Codeara Company.

Last night seven of them arrived at the house. Three of them had been running hard, in an attempt to escape the gunshots of the "cat" (foreman), Cascavel, and the brutalities of Ubirajara—both of whom were accompanied by police. The seven slept and ate here. They will wait until nightfall and then flee, via Isla, to Belém-Brasilia: a journey of 40 leagues, 240 kilometers, on foot! The father and father-in-law of two of them—a 72-year old man with a hernia—is in the clinic, still waiting for the agent, Decio, to fulfill his repeatedly false promises (our beneficent, "paternalistic" solution).

When we asked him why he drank, the poor drunk peon answered nobly: "I drink because of the blues. . . . The people drink to chase away the blues." (Drinking to forget. . .!)

I have just heard that three more peons are planning to run away. . . .

There is no real peace without truth and justice. Any

other kind of "peace" is nothing but a lie, a form of hypocritical exploitation (or cowardly conniving). When Christ gave his peace, he stressed that it was not given as the world gives it. He no doubt had something very definite in mind.

8/18: Canuto and I talked about needed pastoral reforms. We talked about marriages that should be annulled for lack of psychological maturity on the part of the couples, or because of external coercion. Once again, it was the basic, never-resolved problem of the pastoral administration of the sacraments!

Should we just—in all logic and honesty—overlook all our juridical scruples? Should we do so even if the people are not prepared, or have no "fatal" need of the sacraments? What does that leave us with?

The facts are there, staring us in the face: nearly all are baptized; most are ignorant, "indifferent," "incapable" of receiving the eucharist here and now! ("Incapable": By whose standards? And they tell us that the sacraments are to be administered to people who have been "proved ready to receive them"?)

8/19: Fr. Francisco leaves for Brasilia, Campo Grande, etc. He's still a bit nervous. Earlier, we had celebrated his fiftieth birthday (it will be on the 29th of this month). We had dinner and a "cake." There were jokes and some sad truths: Codeara, coops, escapes, diplomacy and *politesse*, reports and denunciations, motions. . . . He is a big kid, this fighting Francisco!

Weariness, fear, and contemporizing can easily become prudence and strategy.

The cause of justice is untiringly stubborn, keenly

lucid, consistent—in all ways—to the very end. Like love. And out of a practical love for men in the concrete (after all, that's the only kind of men that exist).

Justice does not exist. Its causes and its victims exist: the just, the victims of injustice and oppression. But so does the Just One!

Yesterday I offered a "defense" of my longstanding friendship with Therese of Lisieux. I am happy to find her permanently ensconced in my life. She's like a big sister who has already reached happiness. I can count on her, with her "roses" (which are by no means easy) and on the harsh, pure counsel of her life. Thanks, little one! You can only go on pilgrimage in company. You can only live humanly, Christianly, in friendship.

8/21: Tomorrow will already be the Feast of the Heart of Mary. I am beginning to glimpse a whole new outlook on the truth of what Mary means, a new phase of my faith in her, and in my feelings of tenderness for her: the Virgin of the *Magnificat*, the songstress, the prophetess, the exemplar and the guarantee of the Poor of Yahweh. The Virgin of Redemptive Liberation ("contradicted" on the cross). Our Lady of the Passover—the Passover once and for all.

9/13: In Rio and in São Paulo, the "nongroup" of us bishops who are committed to confronting the realities of the church and this country held three meetings.

During this latest trip, I have made a number of impressive contacts. There is a great deal of good will among the persecuted, the outcasts, those who hope for a better tomorrow, building it inch by inch, in "blood, sweat, and tears."

I went to see *Frei Caneca* (Friar Caneca), a very up-to-date piece of theater: "Quem beber da àgua das minhas canecas, fica para sempre com sede de libertade" (Whoever drinks water from my tankards, thirsts ever after for liberty).

9/18: Yesterday two men died in a truck wreck, about three miles from São Félix. I visited the hospital twice. There you can see the *fazendas'* sadly mixed dialectic of oppression and slavery: peons, assistant managers, and foremen; injured, sick: reduced to equality by the common denominator of the suffering human condition.

One Sunday afternoon, I walked through these streets of São Félix. What are we to do for this motley bunch of people (whores, peons, drunks, poor people of all sorts, exploiters, defenseless children, the sick, the unemployed)?

9/25: A general and Colonel Ramalho (God forgive them) and four truckloads and two jeeploads of soldiers arrived in town. Soldiers, weapons, explosives. They have come in search of terrorists. They have come to make "inquiries." (?!)

The colonel has questioned some of my household in gross and abusive terms. He asked me, for example, whether I had "heard anything from Rio de Janeiro," whether I was "scared," whether "I like the army." From the moment he entered, he addressed me either by my last name, or in the overly familiar "*tu*" (Hey, you!). They have requisitioned a room at the school, and are handing out candies and gadgets to the children.

Eugenio came back sick from Serra Nova. Perhaps sunstroke, perhaps an intestinal infection.

The day before yesterday, São Félix finally got electric lights! (For the "main streets," naturally.) And we have been "honored" these days, by the presence of the three candidates for "*prefeito*" (mayor), with their sidekicks and cars and their fatuous showing-off. . . . Also, the day before yesterday, the state secretary of health closed down our clinic and officially opened a "*posto de saúde*" (health center).

9/30: It's been very hot lately. But is it any hotter than in former years? Who knows? The present hot spell, like our present sufferings, always seems greater, because it goes unpublicized.

The soldiers stay on in São Félix, Santa Terezinha, Luciara, Xavantina, Bandeirantes. We're well chaperoned.

The colonel has spoken with me and the rest a number of times. He's a lot meeker, now. He and his companions have had a chance to learn a lot that they didn't know before. The other day, the colonel told me that he had heard a lot of bad reports about me. He later told me that he was getting to find the bishop more "*simpático*," and that he "likes the bishop," although the bishop seems "not to like him."

They're making an effort to say and show that they're here to help, that they just want to make a few little inquiries. We know that they are really in search of their own imagined hobgoblins: terrorists, guerrillas, subversives. And we know that this whole area is being boxed in by an iron grid of the Department of National Security.

A few months ago, there was, in fact, a guerrilla uprising, south of Pará. Naturally, the press was totally silent on the matter. Throughout the countryside the guerrillas distributed an underground letter that was so objective in its description of the social situation in the Amazonian interior that no one in his right mind could disregard it passively.

. . . I had to run off to Pontonópolis, to warn the people about the sophistries of Varjão, a ward heeler who was promising everyone land. The people responded to his preelection publicity with noble skepticism. . . .

We just received a late notice of a visit by Pope Paul to the tomb of St. Celestine. Is the pope going to resign? It would be a beautiful gesture and an example.

10/2: It becomes ever more clear to me that we urgently need someone to remain stably in each place, a small community that would act as a leaven.

10/9: Manuel "passed along a message" by radio, from Goiânia, announcing that Fr. Francisco was in Campo Grande. I can't tell what new turn this unexpected call may signal.

In Santa Terezinha there were four generals present (four!) on our "feastday." Among them was the dangerous commandant of the Second Army, from São Paulo, Humberto de Souza Mello. They obliged Mayor Liton to retract the decree disappropriating the urban area. . . .

The army, as we had supposed, came for an antiguerrilla exercise. And Captain João Evangelista—cynical and sold-out man that he is—has taken advantage of the situation to start some new intrigues against me, regarding the conflict between the *posseiros* and the latifundios.

It's already "winter" down here. I've been a bishop for almost a year, now.

13

10/21: In Porto Alegre, five or six days ago, the *posseiros*—after repeatedly ignored requests to, and endless vexations from, the manager, Plinio, the contractor, Zé Benz, Mayor Liton, the police, and the owner, Dr. Mireilles—cut the wires at the cattle-troughs and along the public highway. Today, very early, Zé Benz brought in two policemen to the Frenova *fazenda*.

I feel tense, but I'm ready to go all the way with this already-martyred town of Porto Alegre.

Perhaps someday the name of Mireilles may be inscribed in the list of *defenders* of "*O Cristo do Povo*" (the People's Christ, as Márcio Moreira Alvez calls him in one book); but today, he'd have to be listed among the *vendors* of this Christ. Once again, money and power have managed to sell the Lord.

10/24: The Frenova people called in the police from Barra to Porto Alegre, and implicated five local men. I wrote a letter of complaint to Captain Moacir. We still don't know the results. I'm sending a copy of the complaint, together with an explanatory letter, to various state, federal, and church authorities.

As I write these lines—on April 21, 1975—I receive a visit from Dr. Medeiros, owner of Frenova and various other great *fazendas* in this region, and one of the four directors of the Amazonian Agro-cattle Association. He is accompanied by a nutrition expert from Massachusetts.

Dr. Medeiros would like "my blessing" on the *fazenda's* project to create a city in Porto Alegre—which would really mean converting it into a *barrio* and its inhabitants into serfs for the *fazenda*. I explain to him that the project is somewhat dubious but that, in any case, the people and not I, must decide. But the outlook is hopeless. The great highway for "Livestock Integration," connecting Mato Grosso with Pará, is going to pass through Porto Alegre. (The skeleton of the bridge over the River Tapirapé is already completed.)

November 1. All Saints. The humanity that God has loved. Those who have responded to Christ. The world free and happy. The history of men joined to the history of God's love. Heaven in heaven. Heaven already on earth.

On October 28 and 29, we held the first meeting for leaders of the future *"comunidades de base"* in the prelature, in the *sertão* of Pontinópolis. It was an interesting experiment in free, fraternal, and simple living-together. As a point of departure for our reflections, we chose the Parable of the Wedding Banquet. . . . The kingdom of heaven was already here on earth, and all of us have been invited to work at building it.

An incident straight out of an espionage novel: Today Dr. Jamil, Seixas of Codeara, Zé Benz of Frenova, and a so-called member of DEOPS all got together to offer their respects (and the use of their cars) to a "friend" from Curitiba, who was recommended to us by the priests there, and who expressed a desire to work with us here. The above-mentioned clique, of course, spoke ill of the bishops, priests, and personnel of the prelature. Convinced that

"Mr. X" was a member of the federal police, nobody could exactly figure out who was who in this scenario.

11/12: Yesterday the Little Sisters, I, and the whole group from Santa Terezinha were in the Tapirapé village, reviewing our personal and communal faith-life. These young people have undergone and are undergoing their faith-crisis. Their faith is both logically self-consistent and abounding in good deeds. Their commitment to humanity and to temporal realities has purified them of any sort of "angelism." The sincerity and generous optimism with which they work for their neighbor inevitably makes them grow closer (since the neighbor is a superefficient sacrament) to Jesus Christ, the Lord.

11/16: When we arrived back in São Félix on the 13th, Ailson, our alleged "friend" from Curitiba, played the opening hand in his dirty game. His real identity is Captain Ailson Munhoz da Rocha Lopes, of the "Military Command for the Repression of Amazonia." He has come to infiltrate our house, because "they" (the army? the government? economic blocs? the devil?—how should I know?) are convinced that we are a center for guerrilla activities and subversion.

Ailson, posing as a soul in search of spiritual direction and as a potential missionary vocation, based his claims on a letter of introduction from the Claretian house in Curitiba. He has managed to come and go as he pleases at our house, although we are not at all convinced of his credentials.

He told us of new control-measures that were being

planned, and he "forewarned" us about possible repri-
sals and judgments. . . . He described Porto Alegre, because of its struggle with Frenova, as a center of suspi-
cions: He would have us believe that an ex-guerrilla
from Valle da Ribeira (who would have loved to sink his
claws into the guerrillas!) was being detained there; and
he identified a "peon" (whom none of the people had
ever heard of) as an alleged agitator with a huge supply
of cyanide at his disposal, as well as a fair-skinned, "different," female companion—like the inevitable "blonde"
in all spy plots. . . .

He proudly claimed that "they" (the military) were the
real power in the country, and that they were "gaining
more and more control of the government." "The end,"
he repeated cynically, "justifies the means." Altair, the
poor, dedicated teacher from Porto Alegre, has had to
disappear once more. . . .

Last night our heads were spinning. God keep us
centered in hope! The townspeople are legitimately dis-
concerted: What kind of group are we, after all?

11/17: I have been reading some magnificent pages by
Boros, on hope, death, and resurrection. "God offers no
'response' to human suffering." It is useless and anti-
Christian to offer any rational justification of suffering.
The cross is not a philosophical category.

11/21: Feast of Our Lady's Presentation. I put some
flowers before the faded statue of our Lady in the
church on the hill.

Yesterday, the state secretary of health arrived with
materials and orders to build a "health center" here in

Santa Terezinha, before the end of the year. One more stretch of the fence being built around the work of our prelature.

"The Bible," says Girardi, "is the history of God's trust in men."

11/28: I am in Porto Alegre. We arrived here the 24th, with Pontin. It was a moment of acute tension for the town. Eugenio, who has become a marvelous "country priest"—worthy of Bernanos, worthy of the Lord—has evidently been a light and a living rock for the people here.

At any moment, they were expecting some violent intervention on the part of Frenova. The last days have been days of humiliation and terror for the people, most of whose lives and rights have already been trampled on.

It was the *fazenda* that brought our alleged friend, "Captain" Ailson, here. (Did they bring him to São Félix, too?) Here in Porto Alegre, he accused various people of being guerrillas, humiliated them, destroyed their pathetic weapons, and—in the *fazenda's* own office—detained and interrogated Fr. Eugenio and various *posseiros*, and brewed up a climate of terror, generally.

At this very moment—a little after seven in the evening—Antonio Camilo is singing a song with some magnificent lines about the *sertão*: a legend of a time and a place that will make history in their own way. The words, the music and his voice are worthy of a troubadour, creating a *chanson de geste* for Latin America.

Pontin returned to São Félix yesterday, bringing with him a detailed and weighty report I wrote on the acts of aggression carried out by Frenova against the people of Porto Alegre during these past years.

I just came back from attending a spectacular "rodeio." On his first try, a twelve-year old boy lassoed a white pony galloping through the green street that we have christened "Avenida de la Libertad." Then the rest of the kids broke the animal in, mounting it wild and bareback, with all the power and joy of country people.

12/12: In Anápolis, from the 4th to the 7th, we had an episcopal meeting of the members of the West-Central Region of the Council of Bishops.

The prelature of São Félix was put to a vote. Could we or could we not remain officially in the Region? There was some behind-the-scenes opposition, but Dom Fernando defended us with his generous, fatherly heart. Could the opposition be based on mistrust of us? Subversives are causing trouble everywhere. . . .

During the meeting, we visited the nearby airport where the Mirage jets are stationed. What an expense to bolster military pride! Each of them costs 16 to 18 million, new. Won't it be beautiful (will it?) when the day comes where men will discover that they can get along without any armaments? What a human world it would be, where men would only have "bases" of roses and lettuce!

From the 8th to the 10th, here in São Félix, we had a general meeting of all the members of the pastoral team of the prelature. (Only the persecuted Altair, and Eugenio, who was on duty at Porto Alegre, were missing.) They were three very full, sincere, and profound days. We closed with a beautiful eucharist: community absolution, the rite of peace, a full communion. We made our options and defined the basic lines we would follow in our pastoral commitments. We discussed the scope of liberation, poverty, faith, and (socio-political) ecumenical action for justice. And we decided to have a general meeting of the team at the end of each semester. The community is growing—sad but free, many but united in common cause—in the Lord. God is with us, and people are praying for the prelature.

We defined the objectives and basic guidelines for the pastoral ministry of the prelature as follows:

The local church of the prelature of São Félix, in communion with the church of Third World,
—for the sake of the gospel,
—and answering the needs of real, local needs,
—opts for the cause of the oppressed.
Consequently, it defines its pastoral ministry as a liberating evangelization, in accord with the inspired Word: "The Spirit of the Lord is upon me, because he has anointed me and sent me to announce the good news to the poor, to proclaim release for prisoners and recovery of sight for the blind; to let the oppressed go free, and to proclaim the year of the Lord's favor" (Is 61: 1-2; Lk 4: 18-19).

In a first analysis, which makes no pretense at being exhaustive, we have singled out the following points as basic elements in the overall problem of the oppression in which the people of this region live:
—superstition, fatalism, and passivity;
—illiteracy and semiliteracy;
—social marginalization;

—the capitalist latifundio (huge landed estates), which perpetuates this condition of oppression.

Our objective: The prelature's objective is to unleash and accelerate, among the people of this region, the process of total liberation wherein Christ freed us (cf. Gal 5).

Our means:

1. Becoming incarnate in the poverty, struggle, and hope of this people.
2. Providing a liberating education to raise the consciousness of the people and to promote human advancement.
3. Prophetic denunciation.

Commitments:

  a) Fully aware of the conflicts implicit in this fundamental option, we are committed to respecting the stages of liberating growth among the people, as well as the pluralism of charisms and ministries.
  b) Respecting the personal options of the different members of the team, we are also committed as an ecclesial group, to an explicit attempt at living our faith—in the witness of our life and in prayer, especially in the celebration of the eucharist—and to a periodic review, comparing our basic option with the concrete action we have taken to fulfill it.

(This page on our objective and basic pastoral approach was later to be submitted as a fundamental piece of evidence against us, in the military trial.)

12/16: I have been writing letters, as well as a short article on conversion, which Teófilo has asked me to submit to *Misión Abierta*. Before a person writes about conversion, he should himself have undergone conversion, which is a radical matter, an everyday matter, involving the whole of ones life....

These days, I have been burning up inside: preoccupations; the impasse of the *posseiro* problem; the tiny "sollicitudo ecclesiarum" of this *sertão;* my own resentful silences and complexes; and, crowning it all, the cross of the Lord.

Christmas is approaching. It will be frugal—almost harsh. May it be Christian!

12/27: I visited Serra Nova on horseback. One hundred forty kilometers round trip. The same friends as always, the same mute tension. And that "fearful" tenacity of a people that need to live. Hours and hours on horseback in the rain. Free hours of field and sky. And the atmosphere of Christmas subtly pervading it all, without public notice, without as much as a liturgy. In naked faith....

1973:

1/2: Just Pedrito and I are here. Yesterday Helio and Moura left. Helio will not be coming back this year; he has to continue his studies in São Paulo. Vaime and Elmo left today with Fr. Francisco, who is carrying the "protocol" we signed with Meirelles, in the name of the *posseiros* of Porto Alegre, after some hard bargaining. Meirelles, loudly protesting in the name of his "Catholicism," was scandalized at my saying that capitalism is a sin, and he threatened to turn me in to the presidency of the National Council of Bishops for saying so. It so happens that this diplomatic, nauseating tug of war with Frenova has only served to convince me all the more that capitalism is, in fact, a sin.

1973 has begun. Without illusions. A plain holocaust. Hope strengthened, soberly. Solitude grows as life does: toward the grand Encounter.

1/7: Yesterday I had a visit from the inspector of the federal police, Wilson Bizzo, a resident of Campo Grande, and his secretary. They were visiting several places in the region. They asked me about the letter I sent to the minister of justice—in 1971!—concerning the conflict between Serra Nova and the Bordon Company. A great deal of water has flowed under the dam since then! They excused themselves on the basis of more urgent priorities.... They had not, by the way, ever known anything about our "Captain Ailson." The inspector suggested that he might be from the National Information Service in some other area....

These days I have been meditating on Volume 71 of "Concilium," dedicated to the role of the bishop and the unity of the church. In it, Carlo Molari has some very good things to say on "the bishop as witness to the apostolic faith": "Faith would likewise be apostolic, if it were an expectation of man's future, based on God's love as manifested in Christ, and made credible today by the liberating love of those who are united with him" (p. 13). "The criterion for witness is always and for all, the same: the Word of God, proceeding from the inner life of the church; the constant action of the Spirit, bringing man to the fatherland of freedom. In this sense, the bishop, as witness to the apostolic faith, is fundamentally the man who listens" (p. 16).

1/22: E., a former student at our "Ginásio," has written us a magnificent, grateful, and aware letter, in which he commits himself to the future of "his people," the people of this *sertão*.

1/25: These last few days I have had a new feeling of freedom, because I have reaffirmed my decision of not going to Spain. Not that I don't feel like doing so, or have forgotten what Spain means to me; but I feel as if I have broken my old moorings. This is my land upon this earth. This is my people. For this land and with this people, I shall walk towards the Fatherland.

Yesterday, as I was reading a book by Boros, I meditated on heaven.

And I made a review of my life and being, from out of the depths of this perennial solitude that accompanies me like a shadowy other self:

I blame you, God, for having made me as I am.
I tolerate you, God, for having made me as I am.
I forgive you, God, for having made me as I am.
I thank you, God, for having made me as I am.

For having made me as I am,
I want to love you, freely,
to put more trust in you
and, more passionately,
—for having made me as I am—
I want to satiate myself in you,
eternally.

14

3/6: I've been outside the prelature for a month. Goiânia, São Paulo, Campinas, Uberlândia, Campo Grande, Cuiabá, Barra. Thousands of kilometers by car. And many meetings, a few surprises, and some sorrow.

In São Paulo we held the National Assembly of Bishops. Very "agreeable." Timid, though, and a bit superficial. On the other hand, it was a good opportunity—in a sort of personal "Lateran Council"—to meet with many friends. I can say that I was received affectionately by the assembly in general. Afterwards, in a number of meetings and chats—with young students, priests, sisters, and professors—I had a chance to experience the interest and hope which has been aroused by our little church of São Félix. Once again. It is humbling, sustaining, committing.

The young people are agreed that a truly revolutionary attitude can only come out of radical, inner conversion. Talking with them, I myself discovered, with renewed intensity, that the structures of capitalism (economic, political, or spiritual) are a form of idolatry, a state of sin and death. One must "become marginal" in order to be free and to set others free.

From these encounters, one piercing, glorious image is stamped on my mind: that of the young Alexandre Vanucchi, who died shortly thereafter, under torture, at the sadistic hands of "the Repression," in a São Paulo jail. This young and generous blood will be the seed of better days for the people of Brazil.

In Uberlandia I encountered a new experiment in self-giving. A group of boys and girls, some of them married couples, are living in a country commune, away from it all, and poor. "Uru," it's called: a prophetic name.

I was called to Campo Grande to testify at the trial of Fr. Jentel. Three and a half hours in the military tribunal. The trial is now entering the phase of judgment and sentencing.

The team is at work, scattered about in various settlements. "Classes" have begun. A new phase has commenced for the communities of the *sertão:* an experiment that gives me comfort and one which I hope will yield a plentiful harvest of benefits for the people of this prelature.

We are at present without a church in São Félix. We had to pull the old one down, before it fell on us. The "Adveniat" Society has agreed, in principle, to help us build a church-house of the people. "Casa de Deus— Casa do Povo de Deus" (House of God—House of the People of God).

O. Mattos says: "Deus fica sempre quando passa: God always stays when he passes by." St. Augustine said: "Timeo Jesum transeuntem—I fear the (unnoticed) passing-by of Jesus." Which one should we choose? Right now, I know that Mattos has at least as strong a point in his favor.

3/8: Once again, Luciara. Lord, will '74 be, at last, the "Year of Luciara"? It ought to be, finally. I have spoken with some friends here and I feel, as I always do when I pass by here, somewhat ashamed. Old man Petrolina— who goes to confession with God—informs me that a short time back, he told the new *alcalde* (mayor): "Talk with the bishop. He's a real city whiz."

The state is also constructing a "Health Center" here. If it were not for the great capitalist superstructure—dictatorship, latifundios, external and internal colonialism—there would be no obstacle to publicly adapting and enlarging the existing, admittedly stop-gap, facilities. It is so easy, momentarily, to deceive the people, especially when one can strangle their conscience, after strangling their liberty!

3/13: Santa Terezinha. . . . Two days in Tapirapé, where Luis and Eunice are happy and with a good outlook for their work. The Little Sister, Mayie Batista, helps them in everything. They have just consulted the linguist, Ione. Marcos, the local *cacique* (tribal leader) and his wife, in solemn ritual, have just daub-painted little Wampurā, which is equivalent to adopting him into the tribe.

Sunday we had a general meeting of the *posseiros'* cooperative. I spoke to them, stressing the importance of the power of the people united in the cooperative, and of the slow, self-sacrificing evolution that the cooperativist mentality requires.

Canuto and I visited some *posseiros* at their clearings, some twenty-five kilometers on foot.

I spoke a good deal with Canuto, these days. As a matter of fact, I've been speaking quite a bit with several members of the team lately. Perhaps I'm getting a better grasp of my mission to listen and to dialogue, to be a stimulus and to provide company. Just "to be" a little, always, with everyone, everywhere. Supporting without demanding, assuming without imposing.

Today I'm writing home. They must be suffering, since they know I'm not coming. It's all mission; it's all grace. God is "company" for everyone; he'll be so especially for them. And this sacrifice of home, people and country will make me more one with these, my people. Every renunciation made for the sake of the gospel is liberating and fruitful.

3/18: I arrived here in Campos Limpos (Ribeirão Bonito) the 16th, after a seven-hour delay. The road is really rotten. Yesterday, twelve kilometers from Matinha, more than fifty cars were stuck in the mud.

The whole place is living in the grip of fear. It seems that the local "boss," Zacarías ("the Carranzist"), had a row with certain *posseiros* and was piqued because some of his egotistical schemes had been thwarted. He walked up to Fr. Manuel, knocked him down, struck him, and, armed with his trusty 38 and a long fishing knife, threatened his life. Manuel, seated at the entrance of the house in his customary, discreet watchfulness, didn't have time to see the blow coming. There he was, stretched out in the street, with Zacarías reaching for his revolver, when Sister Beatriz—always a firm and serene soul—stepped between them, and the "boss" felt suddenly cut off, confused, and at a loss for words.

Yesterday, with many people from Ribeirão and Cascalheira present, I celebrated Mass. I seized the opportunity to form the people's conscience and to explain to them the meaning of this act of aggression, which was just one more episode in the struggle for the liberation of our people.

4/1: Serra Nova is growing and is already becoming complicated. And one great cloud of doubt—even greater, now—hangs over its future: the lack of land. And the Bordon Company, the latifundio, the "system," are the powers that be. They hold sway with their propaganda, their "economic miracle," and many of the blissfully ignorant are taken in by it.

4/3: This evening we arrived with Edgar from Antonio de Freitas' house, halfway between Serra Nova and the Río das Mortes. We met there, last night, with a group of neighboring *posseiros*. The Abdalla Company is expanding its fences, and each new stretch of fence closes out that much more future for the poor of San Antonio and the surrounding country between the Rio das Mortes and El Roncador.

4/4: This morning Eugenio and I visited a good part of the area, house by house. In every house we visited, we were met with the same affection and trust (indeed, too much trust in "the Padres"), and the same misery (sickness, lack of sanitation, insecurity). My heart was choking with rage and compassion, welling up into a tense prayer, a cry.

4/5: Yesterday evening Alita, Eugenio, Edgar, and I sat down on a felled tree trunk by the side of the road that runs by the "clearings." We analyzed the situation and tried to outline a program to deal with it. Later we met with a group of leaders at X's house.

This morning I had a visit from Andrelino, a *posseiro* who has been threatened by Tião, "filhote de tubarão" (that son of a shark), with a total fence-out. Even an outsider can see that we live with an obsession about land. Here, the land-problem is an open wound, a daily pain.

4/8: I arrived in Serra Nova after a trip on foot, on horseback, and by truck—up and down, through rain and fair weather—until six in the morning. There we were: with nursing babies, cowhides, two irritated, splendid pigs, all in unison. Eugenio, Lulú, and I passed by the house of old Raimundo Piauí, lost with his children and in-laws, among the brush and crags of the Serra do Roncador.

The news from Pontinópolis is upsetting. Once more I feel gripped with a desperate desire to do something about it all—some ultimate, nameless thing. It is Lent. Easter is coming again, harsh and glorious. One must be poor, powerless. One must hope against all hope. But it's by no means easy to reconcile my people's urgent survival-needs, with the truth (or mirage) or hope as traditional "Christianity" has represented it. Radical reality can't be so tidily controlled. And love is radical. Lord, guide me. Fill up the roads of this prelature, as you fill them with rain, with sun and with lush, green growth.

4/10: Last night little João Paulo, the son of Zeca, from Pontinópolis, died. One more little *posseiro* who made it to the Promised Land. Doca, his mother—a mother for six days without food or drink—fainted, when she heard the news. . . . All of us here at the house have felt the loss of this child, as if it were the loss of one of our own family. I myself, perhaps because I have been so exhausted and because I was so close to Zeca, was very deeply depressed at this death. I even asked the Lord why the little ones have to suffer and die. . . .

4/18: Yesterday evening we buried poor Zé. He was only twenty, a peon from Ceará, nothing left of him but skin and bones. No papers on him. He died of anemia and malaria, in the Indian Hospital. Zé had been working for the Bordon Company when he, like so many others, caught malaria. Bordon is one great, tragic infirmary these days. Gravely ill, Zé was sent to Dr. Jamil at the hospital here. Both the hospital and the *fazenda* "let him go." The *fazenda* gave him 100 *cruzeiros* . . . "to return to his land"! When he got home, he collapsed in the doorway, a broken man. We attended to him and brought him to Santa Isabel, on the Island. The public transport did not want to take him, alleging that he had tuberculosis. And so, waiting there for a plane to taxi him, he died yesterday morning at six, alone. Dr. Américo, of the Indian Hospital, wept when he heard of it. He says that he has seen so many of his relatives leave Ceará, looking for work or land, and they never come back. . . .

The Araguaia was rising, almost to our feet, almost lapping at the edges of our cemetery. It was case #1000.

I feel powerless, responsible, lost. Some of the latest reactions of the Council of Bishops leave me feeling all the more alone. Am I certain of the line of conduct I'm following? If not, then what's the gospel all about? Why am I a bishop? Should I resign?

I copy down these words of Paulo Freire, from his letters to Rogerio de Almeida Cunha: "Nevertheless, the process of human liberation demands a historic commitment, demands taking the sort of transforming action which involves a head-on collision with the mighty of this earth.

"The greatest, the only proof of true love which the oppressed can offer their oppressors, is to radically withdraw from the latter the objective conditions that

enable them to oppress, rather than just suffering oppression masochistically. This is the only way to
humanize oppressors. And this loving task, which is
political and revolutionary, belongs to the oppressed.
The oppressors, as a class that oppresses, will never liberate their victims, nor will they ever liberate themselves.
Only the weakness of the oppressed is strong enough to
accomplish that.

"In order to think aright in this matter, anyone who
lives in a great metropolis must first become a person of
the Third World.

"To be a man of the Third World means renouncing
the structures of power, the 'establishments' which, in
this world, represent the world of domination. It means
being with the oppressed, with those 'condemned to the
earth,' in an attitude of authentic love, which is not an
attitude of trying to reconcile the irreconcilable: those
who oppress, crush, exploit and kill, with those who are
being oppressed, crushed, exploited and threatened
with death. The time has come when Christians should
be able to make the obvious distinction between true
love and its counterfeits of sadism, masochism or a com-
bination of them. Contrary to what most people think,
the opposite of love is not hate, but rather, the fear of
loving, and the fear of loving is the fear of being free."

4/20: Luciara. We arrived yesterday with Judith. And we
celebrated the Holy Thursday eucharist in an atmosphere of simplicity and poverty.

I attended to the spiritual needs of Jão Paulo's eighty-
four-year old mother. She died early this morning, the
day of the Lord's death. After hours of hoarse breathing, like a worn-out old motor: it reminded me of my
father's death.

This morning I visited the Karajá village. Desolation, And, at the same time, peace. May God accompany them until they reach the Great Village of his glory.

I went to confession to Pedrito yesterday, before coming here. Both yesterday and today I have been examining my conscience. Past sins, continuing infidelity, and these new sins of anger and rebelliousness. To what extent are they justified? Where and when do I go too far? Should I compromise? And what of justice? And of zeal for my oppressed brothers? May the Lord himself be the measure of my poor justice, of my mutilated peace. He, who died to make us free, in his total love!

4/21: The most beautiful day of the year, and the happiest night. The mother vigil of all vigils. Holy Saturday, the Paschal Vigil. We lit the Easter fire outdoors, in the plaza. The water was drawn from the Araguaia. A simple and vital ritual.

I believe in the resurrection in the most concretely realistic sense. It is something that this dehumanized and cruel reality demands.

4/24: Dom Tomás passed by here Sunday. He brought us some enlivening news for the church in Brazil, as well as the final version of the "denunciation-book" on the marginalized condition of the people in the West-Central Region, which several of us bishops living here, have signed.

4/27: President Stroessner of Paraguay is going to stop at the Hotel John Kennedy. The Island and the river are swarming with the military. And the police have been going around questioning everyone—for the nth time—about our mysterious lives.

Thursday we began saying "block Masses," in the rustic shop of a carpenter: worthy of Nazareth.

Are we reaching the people? Are we getting close enough to them? Is there anything putting distance between them and us? Are we poor enough, committed enough? São Félix, as a city, continues to be a pastoral nightmare.

I am reading a good book by Leonardo Boff, on Christ's resurrection and ours.

5/13: Recife. Olinda. Towering palms, baroque rocks, history, hills, and the sea. A whole new landscape all its own, this Olinda-Recife area.

There are some thirty bishops gathered here for a crash-course in renewal: theology, updating on conditions in Brazil, pastoral practice.

Fr. Jentel will be sentenced on the 28th or 29th.

Today is Mother's Day. Tinc un record per ella. I un pregària. Que el Crist li faci de Fill, per mi; que ella em doni generosament. Aquell Dia ens retrobarem per sempre, lliures. (I made a memento for her. And a prayer. May Christ be a Son to her, in my stead; for she has given of me generously. On that day, we will meet again, forever, free.)

Yesterday, when we were supposed to be confronting "Brazilian realities," we went off the track for some time, lost in some of those ambivalent theories that always seem to be tied to "prudence." Life is crying out to us there: in the streets, in the fields!

"I renounce the sea" is one of my "key-poems" relating to these days. And, indeed, the sea was a great temptation: green, blue, and white beyond those ancient rocks, beyond those graceful, lofty palms.

15

5/29: Campo Grande. Yesterday afternoon, around 3:00 in the military tribunal, Fr. Francisco was condemned to ten years imprisonment, "for breaking the law of national security." And yesterday itself, he was locked up in the jail of the military police.

That morning, before going to the tribunal, he and I concelebrated Mass ("The Lord alone is my judge. . . . If they have persecuted me, they will persecute you. . . . Blessed are you when men persecute you. . . .").

I am told that Elmo is in hiding (locked in the Ginásio), because they are plainly out to kill him.

Francisco remains serene and generous through it all.

The feast of Pentecost is approaching, and we must entrust ourselves to the Spirit of Jesus who, by means of us, is working out the sorrowful history of the salvation of men.

On May 30, in São Paulo, I signed a document for the sad occasion: "The Condemnation and Testimony of Fr. Francisco Jentel, Missionary of the Prelature of São Félix, Mato Grosso." The only way I could distribute it was, of course, via the underground medium of a multicopy machine. In the document I made a point of reminding my readers that we happened to be celebrating "in a particularly tragic manner, the twenty-fifth anniversary of the Universal Declaration of the Rights of Man."

6/20: It has rained a great deal lately. Sun, dust, mud, journeys, history, the Passion of Christ and of the people.

Francisco is still in prison at Campo Grande. We also know (although we don't know where, since Pedro Mari

wasn't able to find out in Cuiabá or Campo Grande) that
Terezinha, Edgar, and Teresa—a girl who is a friend of
the Little Sisters and happened to be visiting the
prelature—have also been imprisoned.

Immediately after Francisco was sentenced, the military police, the air force and the army—in a real outburst of vandalism—invaded almost the whole area of
the prelature. Robbing, beating, humiliating, slander-
ing, violating houses and our archives, and carrying
off. . . .

Later, Elmo, in a state of depression, and almost destroyed psychologically, had to leave for therapy.

School has been suspended. The climate is one of desolation and trial.

On July 7 I published another document: "Operations
of the Military Police and Other Armed Forces in and
around the Prelature of São Félix, Mato Grosso." It con-
cluded in these words:

At this hour, with full consciousness and with a total
will, we commit ourselves to the cause of the oppressed
people of this region—especially the *posseiros*, the peons,
and the Indians—out of love for the gospel of Our Lord
Jesus Christ, and in solidarity with all those who suffer
persecution for justice' sake in this country, which is so
bent on economic development and yet so oppressive of
human beings.

*We declare ourselves, in humble gratitude to him who has
deemed us worthy to bear his liberating cross, to be a persecuted
church.*

And however persecuted, slandered, controlled, or
imprisoned we may be, we will continue our work *of*

consciousness-raising and evangelization—which are one and the same work—in all its fullness, for the sake of the church of Christ, which is concerned with the whole man, and not just with "spirits" (contrary to the opinion of the would-be theologian, Colonel Euro).

We recognize our weaknesses; we may even falter some day. But today, we trust in him who is our power.

We ask all those who have joined us in friendship and in prayer, to join us in giving thanks, because we sincerely believe that those are truly "Blessed, who suffer persecution for justice' sake."

Continuing, now, from my diary:

6/30: All of the "survivors" of our prelature team got together to review our situation and our pastoral plans, especially since the beginning of 1974.

A harsh grace, but grace nonetheless. I sense and foresee in all of this a providential purification, and a response by the Lord to a host of my mute callings on him. We will have to be poorer, more evangelical, more total. The fire of persecution has just burnt down the few structures our prelature had. . . .

I think that, commencing from this trial, we will be more authentically evangelizing, without for a moment ceasing to be equally committed to the socio-political realities of our people.

This has been a mighty wind of Pentecost.

7/22: Sunday. I am at the Sisters' house. It is that time of evening—the setting sun, the Araguaia, the solitude—that invites who knows what evocations and hopes—and fears, too.

Little Sister María Olidia is praying, seated on the floor of the improvised chapel: the only "material" church left in São Félix, the "See" of this prelature. One month has gone by, as long as a century. Nine of our number are now in prison. Besides Francisco, Terezinha, Edgar, and Teresa Adão, somewhere (we really don't know where), Pontin, Moura, Tadeu, Adauta, and Lulú are being held prisoner.

Our two houses—the prelature's and the Sisters'—were hemmed in by soldiers carrying machine-guns. All of us, bishop, priests, and nuns, were under house-arrest. Even when we went to say Mass, we were accompanied by armed soldiers.

On the night of the 8th and the 9th, a group of paisano-style officials, led by Airforce Captain Monteiro, made an armed raid on our house. And they dragged off Fathers Eugenio, Canuto, Leopoldo, and Pedro Mari as prisoners.

It was a repressive commando raid: brutal, well-trained, and sadistic. Maybe even under the influence of drugs.

Monteiro gave the order for someone to take off my glasses. I removed them myself. They wanted me to reveal the whereabouts of Pontin and Moura (hidden in the river) and of Leo and Pedrito who had slipped out to warn the others.

I stuck to the line that it was a matter of conscience, and that I would say nothing. At this, Monteiro, in an attempt at banter, said: "He talks very little, but he writes very well." Then, to egg me on, he said: "Afterwards you can publish a report on all of this!"

The four Padres were tied, humiliated, and beaten. Eugenio even vomited blood from the elbow blows he received in the stomach.

Pedrito wept disconsolately when he saw that Pontin and Mouro had been taken.

It was a night of terror. We all felt that the "powers of darkness" had become incarnate in our midst.

"Old" Goiás received us with the same brotherly friendship as always. Dom Tomás, Fragoso, and a group of priests, Sisters, and lay men and women, who had just finished holding their diocesan assembly, joined us in reflecting upon these latest happenings, and helped us work out the position we should take regarding them.

The parish of Vila Operaria (Workersville), in Goiânia, where Leopoldo lives—the house which is a contact for our mission—was also under siege for five days, with agents troubling them persistently. We spent three days in hiding. On Sunday, the police or the army (most probably, the army) held up a flight for an hour, trying to find out if my name was on the plane's roster of passengers. According to the latest disptach from a general in Goiânia, they want to expel me from the country. Naturally, I'll only leave the prelature under force. If I am expelled, I'll come back, if God helps me figure out how to do so. . . .

This may be the last moment. (But then I have feared—and even desired—that other moments would be the last.)

We are going to be tried, officially. It is the hour of our Passion Many friends, acquaintances, and strangers are accompanying us.

There is a strong bond of communion between us and our fellow-prisoners, their families, our persecuted brethren, and the terrified populace: a bond which maintains us in a state of watchfulness and keen-eyed sentry duty. God blesses when he wounds. The fire of persecution is a priceless baptism.

7/31: I begin by copying some words from Díez-Alegría's "I Believe in Hope!" (p. 78):

"As my conscience sees it, remaining in the church is conditioned by two factors: *First,* that a person should not abandon his ethico-prophetic religious stance and that he should continue denouncing the ontologico-cultist religious aberration, and striving to the best of his ability to overcome this aberration, both in himself and in others. *Second,* that he be conscious of the fact that the Catholic church, and all churches that call themselves Christian and take faith in Christ as their starting-point, are called to be converted to the ethico-prophetic religion of Jesus crucified and glorified, which must prevail, in order that history may reach its ultimate fulfillment. And if thee is a calling to, then there is also a hope for, conversion. At what price, God only knows. . . ."

Yesterday and the day before, for sixteen hours, I had to testify at the police "inquest" which has been opened against the prelature team. Pedrito had to answer questions a day earlier; as Canuto had to, two days earlier, in Santa Terezinha; and as Eugenio must, here, today. Presiding over the "inquest"—by direct orders from Brasilia—is the chief inspector of the federal police in such matters, Francisco Barros de Lima, from Goiânia.

All of those in prison are now at Campo Grande. "At present," says Dr. Francisco, "they are doing well." Sister Judith has left today on a "samurai" mission, to visit them, to bring them clothes and, above all, Communion.

The whole trial will be brought to term in the military tribunal at Campo Grande. Yesterday, I insisted on being included in the common trial with the rest. Dr. Francisco said that he'd present my petition to Brasilia. It's a sad privilege, being a bishop!

What we are really being asked to do, when you get right down to it, is to admit that our "prophetic" activity is a crime, and to promise that we won't continue it in the future. "Judge for yourselves. Should we not rather obey God than men?"

Colonel Euro, sullen as ever, was in Santa Terezinha, threatening to bring in a military chaplain on the case— the way you'd "bring in" a doctor or a detective on a case! Besides being a self-styled "theologian," it seems that the colonel would now like to act the part of vicar general.

I have been writing home, and singing about freedom.

My poem, *"El nom novell"* (Catalán for "The New Name"), came to me during the trial, as I was writing home to my mother. It reads as follows:

Tears, silence, cries—
these words that fill
my mouth and mind.
Not until now, mother,
had I come to grasp
the meaning of
lib-er-ty!

(With all who fought and died for her,
with all who sing and suffer, and who dream of her,
I sing and suffer
—even win a crumb—
of free, free liberty!

I mean that fullest freedom, mother
—Christ's—which sets us free at last.)

If someday I am christened once again
in the water of choking tears and memory,
in the fire of death and Victory,
Tell God and tell the world
that you have given me
the name of
Pedro-Liberty!

8/3: Dom Tomás and some other friends have spent the night with us. Yesterday afternoon, Eugenio and Tomás flew to Porto Alegre in their little "put-put." Diomar and Altair are on the alert in the "*mata.*"

The federal police are in Serra Nova. His health recovered, our good Lulú just set out for Serra Nova today. He arrived here yesterday, like a present from heaven. He has suffered much, as have all our imprisoned members. Last night, at our deeply moving Mass in the cartman's house, we meditated, once again, on the comforting episode of Peter's imprisonment and release, in Acts.

8/4: Yesterday afternoon Manuel, Vaime, and Luis Goya arrived at the house of Luis Jacaré, on the Island. They were bringing the Sisters' van. Pedro Mari and I went to speak with them. Luis and Vaime were full of greetings. They return today to Goiânia, where they and the rest of the team will be interrogated, sometime around the middle of this month.

As we were returning to São Félix after dark, the reflection of the city shimmered in the river, like a high-branched candle holder, melting in the water.

Manuel has brought in more letters, more messages of

support. I get the impression that they think there are more of us than there really are, and that they are expecting too much of us. We will have to be faithful to the exaggerated confidence of these friends.

I am writing a letter to the people of the prelature, inviting them to a concelebrated Mass on the 19th. Fifteen bishops are already coming for sure.

8/7: This morning, Sister Irene and I went through the streets distributing the letter of invitation. There weren't enough letters for everybody: just for the poorest. The people received us with grateful affection, and now they're looking forward to the great concelebration with a naive hope that hopes too much. After all, the coming of fifteen or twenty bishops can only mean that they're going to solve all problems once and for all. . . . In the tormented brains of this beloved people, "authority" is still a myth.

Among the badly handled (perhaps opened?) letters that arrived today, there was one from Jordi C. i P., a former student of mine in Sabadell. He is writing to me and is going to write to the pope.

Poor Sister X. has become completely unbalanced. The mental scars of her infancy, to begin with, and then, perhaps, others. May the Spirit of Jesus be with her on her way.

The days are getting to feel as long as those of a sick man.

. . . How solidly and freely the "humility-truth" of Teresa of Jesus seems to be growing these days!

Tomorrow is the feast of Lawrence the Martyr, from Huesca. . . .

On the 19th, the liturgical feast of the Assumption, patroness of São Félix, "on the banks of the ritual river, the Araguaia," we celebrated the great *Eucharist of Solidarity.* Besides the nineteen bishops who were there personally or by proxy, and had expressed their effective collegiality in a moving document, eighteen other bishops, who were meeting at Manaus, also sent a message.

The federal police took photos, drawings, and notes of the whole ceremony. "They" passed out pamphlets bearing the exotic emblem of a cross and sickle, allegedly signed by the "Communist Party" and the "progressive church." They were also busy spreading rumors and threats. Despite all this, the people rose to the occasion and attended in great and moving numbers, so that they received that interecclesial concelebration like a confirmation in hope.

For us, it was a new witness to the "communion that ventures as far as commitment." On the 3rd of October I published a report: "The Prelature of São Félix, Mato Grosso—between Trial and Solidarity." It ends in these words:

"This manifold show of solidarity moves us and commits us, like an expressive sacrament of ecclesial communion, to liberating hope and human corresponsibility in the struggle for justice. Through it, we feel we hear a new call from the ever-demanding Word of God.

"The friendship, prayer and expectations of our brothers has been for us a living proof of the presence of the Lord Jesus, who is always there, where two or three are gathered in his name. And we are gathered here out of love for him, for the sake of the gospel, to progressively bring about—in this first, earthly and conflict-ridden phase of his reign—the new life of the children of God, who are all equal and free, with that liberty wherein Christ liberated us" (Gal 5:1).

16

9/3: Terezinha, Tadeu, Moura, Pontin, Edgar, and Teresa are free now, at least provisionally. I met them all in São Paulo. They were effusive, but marked by their ordeal: more conscious of their faith and of the commitments it entails. They have suffered greatly. They were brutally tortured, badgered, and humiliated. Their captors wanted to wrench false confessions from them, e.g., that we belonged to some subversive party or organization, that the priests were having sexual relations with the girls, etc.

Poor creatures, they've been heroic. And they have left a good odor of Christ in the church of Campo Grande, as I learned when I visited Fr. Francisco there, last Sunday, the 5th.

The young people, boys and girls, are all planning to return to the prelature. I don't know to what extent this will be possible, but come what may, their courage and their resolution are a comfort to me.

9/18: The military peace-making force—General Tasso, Colonel Meireles, and other lesser state functionaries— have visited us these days. A total zero. Nothing but publicity and demagoguery. Colonel Meireles showed all the people a series of slides of the highway from Cuiabá to Santarém, for which he is responsible. (As if to show the other, service-oriented face of that army which had already proved here what capable cutthroats and vandals they can be!) As the *pièce de résistance* of their show, the land-merchant and landowner, Ariosto, said that he would give ten thousand hectares of land to the people of Pontinópolis. (In fact, at this late date in 1975, the people of Pontinópolis have received nothing. Moreover, Ariosto was "giving" what he didn't own. In compensation he gained an infinite stretch of 2 million hectares in the Cuiabá-Santarém area in Teles-Pires. He paid for part of it. He could well afford to. . . .)

The problem of education continues on the same low plane. We can manage to make it to the end of the year, plugging up the same old holes.

Allende has been assassinated in Chile. Paul VI has lamented "the tragic military coup." Brazil has rushed to be the first to recognize the new military dictatorship of Chile. Liberty is getting to be a difficult thing to find in this young and irreversible America.

I have written to Fr. Leghisa (superior general of the Claretians), to his consultors, and to all the Claretians gathered for the general chapter in Rome.

9/25: I am in Serra Nova. The mayor's office continues to shirk its duties. The highway is a shambles. Once again, these 300 families are stranded, without an exit, during the rainy season. And all those potentially and certainly sick cases here!

10/19: After many denials and delays (on the part of the scheming local authorities), a place was finally found in Vila Nova, where we may construct our new church—the "cathedral"—of São Félix.

It's "official visiting time" again. The army, air force,

and military police are recruiting. Making the rounds with "Projeto Rondo" from the universities. They fill the streets and public places of our prelature. Pulling teeth by the bushel, they also hope to pull in some admirers.

Three days ago, as we were coming from Barra, Eugenio and I were searched—suitcases, pockets, documents, papers. Yesterday Teodoro (the "gaucho" priest who's been helping us this season) was also searched, on his way back from Serra Nova. They stole one letter and another four or five documents.

Today two reporters came to interview me, one from the *Jornal do Brasil,* the other from *O Estado de São Paulo.* Through them I learned of the criticisms leveled against us by Colonel Meireles and Gabriel Müller (the governor's representative here). Steps are being taken to set up "Operation Araguaia" in this region: a permanent welfare (and repression) program, to counteract the pernicious influence of the clergy, or, as the press of the country is now putting it more neatly, "to minimize the action of the clergy."

A short time ago, during this new and picturesque phase of "smoothing out ruffled feelings," I am told that the head of the federal police went so far as to accord me a certain amount of praise in the presence of the archbishop of Brasilia (as Golbery himself did, later!?). Clearly, one would like to hear and see something better than diplomatic eulogies.

10/25: I feel like fleeing, but won't. The "everyday" is the test of fidelity: the martyrdom of our vulgar, day-by-day existence.

The Lord is my judge, and I can't presume to boast of

anything, honorably. It will be a very good day indeed,
when he forgets both my good deeds and my bad deeds.
I can by no means boast of my justice in his presence.

During the tense days of the "inquest into subversion,"
when my companions were imprisoned and the outlook
was dark and gloomy, I wrote this poem:

> *Lord Jesus!*
> My force and my failure:
> You are.
> My inheritance and my poverty.
> You, my justice,
> Jesus.
>
> My war
> and my peace.
> My freest freedom!
>
> My death and my life,
> You.
> Word of my cries,
> Silence of my waiting,
> Witness of my dreams,
> Cross of my cross!
> Cause of my bitterness,
> Pardon for my selfishness,
> Crime of my trial,
> Judge of my poor weeping,
> Reason for my hope,
> You!
> My Promised Land
> You are. . . .

The Passover of my Passover:
our glory
forever,
Lord Jesus!

17

11/5: I have been in Santa Terezinha. With Tadeu and Terezinha, our accountants at the cooperative, who are going to get married on December 31, "taking the leap" on St. Sylvester's day. A new married couple "from" the prelature.

I said All Souls Day Mass at Luciara. And I managed to exert some control over the "spontaneous" project for building the new church. "X," who is always so diplomatic, with the clerical background he picked up as a seminarian in the north, in the good old days, actually took it for granted that Codeara would go for the plan. Blessed be God and the spirit of Fr. Jentel! "X" even wanted to ask for help from the other *fazendas* of the township. It reminded me of those palmy days of the huge Christs and pietàs, "paid for by rich adulterers and exploiters of the people"—as we used to say at cursillos and in mission sermons. . . .

The walls of the new church for São Félix are going up. It's building time. Hopefully, it is time for living buildings! I hope that the fascination for rocks or bricks will not tempt us away from our passion for men, living stones. At any rate, each place needs a gathering place where people can encounter the Word, pray, and share the eucharist.

11/30: St. Andrew's Day. He loved the cross, that hard and certain "spes unica" (only hope).

Yesterday I returned by autocar (with breakdowns), after fifteen days of roving about in this up-to-date ministry of *"encuentros."* No doubt about it: meeting one's brothers and sisters is a great help in deepening our mutual communion.

The nuncio received me almost respectfully.

I don't believe it's irreverent or anarchistic of me to say that I wish they'd close down the "Vatican" and nunciatures. . . . The pope needs an advisory and secretarial "curia," but not precisely a "state." There could still be "nuncios," although they might not be necessary after all, in view of the existing Conferences of Bishops and the decentralization and "lower-keyed" trend in the church today. There could be nuncios, yes, but of a different sort and style.

This is what I'd like and what I seek. And I do so with much love for the church of Jesus, and in close communion with Paul VI, now heroically "reigning." May his reign be ever less of this world and more and more for the good of the gospel and of mankind.

Francisco is waiting. I have visited him at Campo Grande. Around the end of October he went through a pretty low period, waiting in vain for a response from the Military Superior Court. I spoke about this with Cándido Mendes, president of the National "Justice and Peace" Commission, and with Dom Aloísio and Dom Ivo. They feel that if the court handed down a decision just now, it would confirm and probably increase Francisco's sentence.

That's how it goes during this interim period, awaiting the "advent" of Geisel. Hot-and-cold. Under the table deals and bureaucratic vendettas, on the part of those who are leaving power. . . .

We have been receiving more-or-less contradictory, basically tragic, reports from Chile. The new overlords of Chile are persecuting and killing at will. Yesterday, in *Documents d'Església*, I read the testimony (martyrdom) of Fr. Joan Alsina, of Girona, who was killed in Santiago for having remained faithful to his mission as a priest-worker. The church of Latin America is faithful in its "hour."

12/5: I am in Porto Alegre. While I was visiting Diomar's "orchard"—already densely planted with mandioca, bananas, beans, corn, and rice—we ran into a large, black and dangerous *"jararacuçu do breijo."* It was the fourth "cobra" they had seen that day. They also tell me that the onças (small tigers) have been roaming about the local clearings, since they are being displaced by the fences of the *fazendas*.

The Frenova group is almost demoralized, as well it might be. The latest of its many feats was to fence in the Tapirapé River with four lines of wires. All we need to have them do now, is to fence in the sky, and set their cows to graze on clouds!

12/12: Santa Terezinha. Tapirapé. Last night we celebrated Mass and used the letter from our two exiles, Chico and Rosa, as a reading.

The desert and exile. A somewhat new theme—at least put together like that—for my meditation and my life. It is a theme for those brave spirits who still wish to be free in today's world.

1974. 1/13: The spaces in my diary are getting larger. . . .

Life goes on, despite the cloud of doubt that hangs over our work and over the people of this region, who are condemned to the latifundio. A new health-cooperative called UNICAS has opened in Santa Terezinha. A new Sister, Edna, a nurse, has come to work there. Conflicts over land continue here and there throughout the prelature, and we follow them very closely, informing and supporting the *posseiros.* Pastoral theology, properly so-called, is becoming more "popular," and at the same time, more critical. (Popular religious piety, its pros and cons, is one of the main topics of pastoral reflection in Latin America, and it's even caught on here.) Geisel's government is about to take power, and this has given rise to God-knows-what naive expectations among some of the official leaders of the Brazilian church.

18

1/18: Arturo Paoli's *La perspettiva politica di San Luca* (St. Luke's Political Framework), together with his previous book, *La radice dell'uomo* (The Root of Man), are to be commended highly. From the latter, I copy the following paragraphs:

"If we instill a spirit of fear or veneration, it means that we are sill working from within a framework of power. . . .

"We should spread the notion that *relating* is difficult.

"We will not achieve our goals through masochism or victimization, since the creation of the person is a long and arduous task.

"It's not all so bad that celibacy is regarded as a non-value today, that it is not only underestimated, but even devalued within church structure itself. It cannot be accepted except as an emptying, humiliation, poverty. Only thus, despoiled of all the cultural "magic" and aggressive rhetoric that have heretofore bolstered it, can it be understood by anyone who lives within a history which has been destroyed by its own contradictions.

"The Gospel (of Luke) tries to instill three ideas in us: the idea of watchfulness, the idea of poverty, and the idea of childhood. . . ."

1/24: It is not hard to understand that the church must become more truly simple, more truly a servant church. To understand the opposite seems hard to me. The New Testament, the example of the first popes and bishops, and the *sensus ecclesiae* all speak out loud and clear on this point.

The "temporal power" of the church, and especially of the papacy, has been an historic misfortune, a misery, a chastisement. It seems that the Spirit of Jesus has decided that now is the time to purify his spouse of this "worldly" wound.

A good distinction: between the church's "communitary" constitution and its "societal" temptation. As González-Ruiz puts it: the church is not a "power"; it is a "force," in the Spirit. The church is not a perfect society: it is a perfect mystery of love, now dwelling imperfectly in the lives of men during their earthly pilgrimage, yet also in the perfect glory of Christ, its head. But although the church is also an institution, it is more hope than institution.

St. Cyprian remarked that "the bishop is in the church and the church in the bishop." Yet he added roundly: "I do not wish to do anything according to my own views, without first taking into account your consensus and that of the people."

According to Boros, the only convincing proof of the existence of God is the life of human beings who truly love their neighbor.

4/8: More than two months have passed without a note in my diary. Could it be that I've said all I had to say? Or is it, rather, that I have begun to live a stage of silence, of more discreet living? History, our history, has in fact become more discreet, more underground. Like the good seed. Please God.

These days I have been trying to prepare my book for the series: The credo that has given meaning to my life. I think I'll call it: "I believe in the freedom of the sons of God!" Writing this book—an autobiography of my own faith—will serve as a humble and grateful review of my whole life's journey in the grace of God. It will also allow me to give my small witness to freedom and hope. I have placed this book in the hands of Mary, and beneath the fire of the Spirit.

It is already Holy Week. Once again, the Passover. Always the Passover. More and more each time, the Passover of the Lord Jesus!

5/3: Brasilia. I have been dancing around for three weeks now: from São Félix to Goiânia to Brasilia to São Paulo to Campo Grande and back—all on account of the judgment of Francisco in the Superior Military Tribunal. It was interrupted, by petition of General Rodrigo Otavio. And from behind, or from above, negotiations between the embassy and the nunciature have been

pressured to have Francisco leave the country. Diplomatically self-expelled, we might say.

As I see it, this is a dirty game of diplomacy, both on
the part of the nunciature and the French embassy. But
I'm not going to go into their intentions. Let us just
suppose that they are ... diplomatic, simply diplomatic.
Diplomacy is not the most adequate forum for the
church of Jesus.

I am told that Delfim Neto, Andreazza, and Buzaid
are under house-arrest. Rumors in high places. It seems
that a crude attempt is being made in the courts and in
public opinion, to set things straight about the case of
Ana Lydia. [It was later established that a son of Minister
Buzaid and a son of Senator Enrique Rezende were involved in the girl's murder.] Power is often a dirty business.

I have been reading, in *El Ciervo,* a chronicle-review
on Marcel Légaut, professor and shepherd. His last
book, *Search, Failure, and Fullness,* appears to contain
some magnificent autobiographical meditations on
faith, prayer, fruitful failure, poverty of life ("not being
anything, just being"), death and hope. . . .

The Guadalupe Press of Argentina, which is in the
final stages of preparing my *Tierra nuestra, Libertad* (Our
Land, Liberty) for printing, has just sent me a warm
letter from Ernesto Cardenal, accepting the task of writing a foreword to the book.

The happiest news of this May: Two Sisters of St.
Joseph are going to take charge of the Indian Hospital
at Santa Isabel on the Ilha do Bananal, as nurses. [As
things turned out, only one Sister came. And now, as I
add these lines in retrospect, towards the end of April,
1975, I can report that she, too, was removed a week

ago, by order of the higher-ups in the Aeronautics Department. They're always doing something to prejudice the cause of the Indians. This has come as a particularly hard blow to me, since the presence of Sister Mercedes at the Indian Hospital, so near to the Karajá village, was a dream I had long cherished. . . .] Once more a new era of patient love and concerned charity has begun for the Karajá Indians, who have been so maltreated by the disintegrating policy of "Integration." I believe most passionately in this native mission.

5/15: Nothing yet on Francisco's trial. Last Wednesday, Civil Judge Alcides Carneiro requested a "look" at the case. Perhaps because the sentence was probably going to be condemnatory. It seems the judge assigned to try the case is "liberal," as they say here. How impatient poor Francisco must be about it all.

Y-Juca-Pirama ("He Who Must Die"), an urgent manifesto in defense of the Indians, signed by a group of us missioners who are particularly sensitive to the issue of this "lost" cause, has just appeared. It is a sufficiently incisive and urgent paper. Another paper, on the Meeting of Tribal Leaders at Diamantino, has also come out.

The cause of the Indian is getting closer to me, these days.

Two happy and friendly Xavante Indians have eaten here at the house for almost a week. One of them, Ataú, has just passed through, with his long black hair, his once fine but now worn physique, and his air of roguish knowledgeability concerning life, men, and institutions. As he says, he only pays attention to "friend"; he has no time for "windbag". . . .

These nights, with Pedrito, we have been discussing (as we used to do in the good old days of our theological fervors) the mystery of the resurrection: the future of matter, resurrection immediately following death, the ideas of Teilhard, Christ's own resurrection, the assumption of Mary. . . . Obsessive themes that I would love to discuss with some good theologian. Themes which nobody really understands, in the long run. . . . Mystery of faith, hope of our life. One day we'll see.

At any rate, I believe in the glorification of the universe. I don't know how, but I believe it must happen. (During the trial, I had also written "Spanish, which sings, or raves, or rambles aimlessly." It was a kind of farewell to the "white heron," to that friendly nature which had accompanied and inspired me for so many years. A farewell that was also a sort of Teilhardian "Little Profession of Total Hope.")

Eunice has arrived here with little Wampurā, who is sick: flu, whooping cough, worms, anemia. . . . A "tribute" to the service of both parents and child to the Indian cause. In today's issue of *Opinião* (6/3/74), I have been reading the interview between Glauber Rocha and Gustavo Dahl (the director), on the movie, *Uirá:* a denunciatory film dealing with the tragedy, and the future, of the Indian. Dahl remarks: "In the New World, from the Bering Strait to Tierra del Fuego, the Indians have been waiting patiently for five hundred years, to civilize us. They are just now beginning to give up hope."

. . . Fr. Francisco was absolved of guilt by the Superior Military Tribunal. After he had spent a year in prison, "revolutionary" justice had finally decided to recognize that he wasn't really a subversive, to cancel the rest of his ten-year sentence, and to remand his case to "common" justice. There are many forms of justice: common justice, military justice, just justice . . . and the justice of God. It is to the last that we appeal, contrite and hopeful.

Francisco is now in France. Free, at last. The poor man had ardently yearned for freedom. Will he return? When? How?

His trial ended with a melancholy lack of foresight, since the real cause of our total trial was left, exasperatingly, untouched: the people continue to be without land and without any hope of land, their rights and aspirations trampled on by official policy and the privileges of the great, which are one and the same thing.

On June 18, I issued a paper, "The Cause, and Hope, Continue," which expresses quite clearly, after due deliberation on the occasion and the words employed, the prelature's reaction to the final outcome of Fr. Jentel's trial, which was mysteriously maneuvered by various diplomatic forces working hand in glove, forces which chose to ignore both my own opinion and the significance that their maneuvering might have in thwarting a more critical and evangelical solution:

"Condemned to ten years imprisonment by the military court at Campo Grande, in a farcical judgment handed down on May 28, 1973, Fr. Francisco Jentel, a priest of this prelature of São Félix, has now, on May 22, 1974, been unanimously acquitted by the Superior Military Tribunal in Brasilia.

"Since the 'crime' of Fr. Francisco was not 'subversion'

or 'communism' or 'guerrilla activity,' then we might well ask: What exactly *was* the sentence handed down by the military court at Campo Grande?

"By its unanimous acquittal, the Superior Military Tribunal publicly recognized that Fr. Francisco had unjustly suffered a year of imprisonment: military justice had condemned military justice.

"This is not the time or place to add a single more explicit word on this matter.

"Let us state here, once more, our solidarity with Fr. Francisco, his elderly mother, and all his family and friends. He, although he is now in France, is very near us. In friendship and in prayer, we are always with him.

"We profoundly regret, indeed, that he was unable to visit us, as we had all been hoping, and as the people of Santa Terezinha had so well deserved.

"No one here regards this liberation of Fr. Francisco as a total liberation. . . .

"And certainly none of us here regards it as a just solution for his cause: for the cause of the church of São Félix is not just the 'personal' cause of Fr. Francisco Jentel. The real cause of Fr. Francisco—which is the cause behind the trial of the pastoral team of the vicariate, and the cause of the church of São Félix—is that of the basic human rights of the people of this region, who have never been attended to but have, on the contrary, always been treated contemptuously, and hypocritically put off with threats of subversion and with cheap welfare handouts.

"And, because it is our cause, our struggle will go on.

"We would like to ask all authorities—civil, judicial, military, diplomatic, and ecclesiastical—who are more or less interested in this case, not to be misled themselves or allow the people to be misled.

"Justice has not been served by this strange liberation of Fr. Jentel. He is just one more victim. Nothing that truly needed resolving has really been resolved. At best, the only thing that has been resolved was one more tension between the 'official' Church and the national government.

"Diplomacy only safeguards the interests of the rich. Justice alone safeguards the rights of the people.

"And the gospel is not diplomacy.

"All can be salvaged, they tell us, by peace; whereas all might be lost by war. Yet the worst war would be better than a false peace, bought at the price of hypocrisy, naiveté, or sins of omission.

"I cannot believe in these new dialogues, carried on by third parties at the top of the pyramid, when the base, the people—who ought to come first—have neither a place nor a voice in the dialogue.

"There are dialogues whose only purpose is to buy silence.

"If my words strike someone as rude or intemperate, I would remind him, for the hundredth time, that the basic problem of land continues, unchanged, throughout the entire area of our prelature. I am talking about what I know and live with daily.

"In all of La Ilha do Bananal, San Antonio, Barreira Amarela, the banks of the Rio das Mortes, Ribeirao Bonito, Cascalheira, Barreiro, Piabanha, Matinha, Serra Nova and its surrounding high plains, Chapadinha, Luciara, São Félix and environs . . . the *sertanejos* or *pos-*

seiros have neither land nor expectations of a human future.

"The very village of the Tapirapé Indians, where Fr. Francisco had come to work some twenty years ago, still has insufficient land, and even that is not properly marked off by set boundaries. The maps and records affecting the case have mysteriously disappeared from the files of FUNAI, on four separate occasions. The work of demarcation has barely begun in Santa Terezinha, and already the people are living in fear that their downtown area will be fenced in at the limits of its existing buildings. No one will be able to tie a horse to a hitching post in front of his house. . . .

"Meanwhile the great cattle *fazendas,* stimulated by government incentives, are growing in number, power, and arbitrary acts of encroachment. And the many written or spoken complaints—whether they proceed from the bishop's segregatedly immune denunciations or from the timid representations of the people—are systematically ignored.

"I hope that those who are responsible will not claim ignorance of the problems of this hacked-up region. . . .

"To all our brothers and sisters in the communion of the faith or in suffering for justice's sake, who have accompanied us so lovingly, both inside and outside Brazil, I would like to repeat what I wrote on May 27, to the church of Campo Grande, which was closest to Fr. Francisco during his year in prison: 'Although the diplomatic manner in which the case of Fr. Francisco has unfolded—diplomatic on the part of nearly all its principal actors—has not exactly been a joyful witness to the gospel, nevertheless the fraternal manner in which this church of Campo Grande has accompanied Father during his imprisonment is a joy and a witness that have compensated for it. We are still counting on your Christian solidarity, because the true cause of the trial continues: our people without land, without a future....'

"The cause goes on, and hence, I repeat, the struggle goes on. And certainly, hope goes on.

"It is not we who have dictated God's plan for human history:

"'I have heard the outcry of my people ... and have come down to rescue them,' says the Lord (Ex 3:7–8).

"'You are all brothers' (Mt 23:8); 'love one another as I have loved you,' says Jesus (Jn 15:12).

"Then he who sat on the throne said, 'Behold! I am making all things new!' (Rev 21:5).

"It is the Spirit of Jesus, the liberator, who wills that his church be committed to the total liberation of man. It is he who requires of this little church of São Félix a tenacious and risk-taking commitment to the marginal man—*posseiro*, Indian, or peon—who makes up the people and forges the human history of these *sertões*."

19

8/20: In his diary, *May Your Feast Never End,* Roger Schutz writes, for August 20, 1969:

"Twenty-nine years ago today, I discovered the village of Taizé. In the community, I have always preferred that nothing special be done to commemorate this day. From the beginnings of Taizé, in this isolated place, day after day, I have kept before me the vision of man, with or without God, as victim of the powerful."

It has also been several years since the awareness and

presence of man, the victim, began to make its mark on my life. Particularly during these seven years in Mato Grosso.

These last weeks I have felt more than usually depressed at the dead end which traps the *posseiros* of this region and of Brazil in general. They have no other alternative: either they become peons, or they accept the ridiculous penalty and launch out with this passport to nowhere, along the streets of misery.

We have thought, discussed, prayed. And we still don't know exactly what to do. In any case, we'll go on here. In hope. Making justice a life-and-death cause. In him who is the just one.

The house is always full of guests, visitors, crying babies, and confidences. Crushing heat. Occasionally, anguish. And "we occasionally venture an answer or a way out that we know is not really possible.

The Risen Christ lives in the glory of the Father and, consciously or unconsciously, in the heart of every man and in the center of the world and its history.

8/21: Tomorrow used to be—still is, perhaps, in some traditionalist communities—the feast of the Heart of Mary. The Virgin of Nazareth. The Virgin of Bethlehem. The Virgin of Calvary. The Virgin of Pentecost. The Virgin glorified with Christ in the living church. Her faith, her total fidelity, her openness to the Spirit, her self-surrender to her Son and to her sons.

9/2: We have returned from Meruri. With us came little Wampurā, lively as a spark, almost a grandson to me in affection. I instinctively imagine some worthy future for him, a struggle for justice and freedom. I would like to see him—now here, now there—enlisted in some liberating cause: perhaps the cause of the Indians, among whom he is growing up, free and loved. Along with Luis and Eunice, came the Little Sister, Mayie Batista.

We had attended the first regional Native Pastoral Encounter, sponsored by CIMI (Native Missionary Council) and celebrated in the Bororo village of Meruri. This was to be the first of six regional encounters in various native areas of the country, culminating in a national encounter. And what we hope and pray is that these meetings will be the beginning of a new, native approach to Pastoral. "*Y Juca-Pirama*" (he who must die), must live. He won't, without a struggle. There are many interests and disinterests that threaten the future of the Indian.

By any standard, the encounter at Meruri was profound and exciting. We—the missionaries—were accompanied by a Bororo chief and a Xavante chief.

On the day before the end of the meeting, we had a celebration—Mass and dances—in the patio, at night, which impressed us all deeply. It will be hard for me to forget the Communion I received from the hand of a ritually vested and painted Bororo. Tomás and I—as bishops, representing sacred authority—were honored with brilliant crowns of macaw and royal hawk feathers, a "boriko," and had our faces painted red with urucum. "*In sanguine*," Tomás whispered to me, as the Indian woman anointed us, with her red and good-smelling hands.

Old Coqueiro—the saint of the tribe, who was practically one of the risen, since he had managed to escape death from a severe case of tuberculosis—told me what he said he had never told anyone else: the genesis tradition of his tribe. It was an encounter with a man of faith. "I knew all of this," he informed me, "—God, the creation of man, the life to come. When the fathers spoke, I believed."

It's beautiful, the notion of God's providence and prevision. God creates man—after creating man's house— and he calls him out of nothing, from within the house, to life, to the world, precisely at the hour of sunset. . . . Outside, in front of man's house, there remained, like a vestige of God, a luminous circle of rainbow. The universe and the roads of man were there, and he was called.

9/4: A sudden gale collapsed the church at Luciara, just as it was ready to be roofed.

We are waiting for Canuto. At any rate, the two letters he has sent us confirm the tragic prediction that has been weighing on the *posseiros.* INCRA says that it is prepared to defend "titled property." A wise capitalist myth, that of private property, sacredly untouchable, its title recognized despite every misery and every other human right. Someone was once scandalized, when I wrote in a pastoral letter, that it was necessary to "demythologize private property." The facts only confirm me each day in my belief. There are other rights that are prior and superior. One might also reverse an old adage, fraught with old prejudices and innate egoisms, and say that "my property only begins where the property of others begins." I can only have, if my neighbor, too, can have.

A lawyer from INCRA—not a very honest one, to be sure, who was later expelled from the Institute— upbraided me, as if it were an accusation stemming from our influence, for an answer he constantly heard from harried *posseiros:* "God made the land for all." This is nothing but the wise, elementary, commonsense meaning of God and of human rights.

9/16: A lawyer and three law-students from São Paulo have been here for a week. Together, we worked out a basic, popular statement to shout out our crying needs (since there is nothing else we can do) so as to provide the people with a new weapon in the arsenal of their stubbornness. These young men were touched by the social realities in which the *campesino-posseiro* lives, as well as by a church with a different image, one they had not known existed.

They had come under the auspices of the group for nonviolence. And this gesture, in the context of my decision or recognition, came as a new impetus to the policy of reconciliation which the Justice and Peace Commission and some bishops are trying to establish with me, after the "diplomatic" exit of Fr. Francisco....

Rain again. With a tornado.

The director of the Guadalupe Press in Buenos Aires wrote to tell me that, finally, Ernesto Cardenal's foreward to my book of poems (*Tierra nuestra, Libertad*) had arrived. It was a letter in verse which, Fr. Gallinger assured me, was well worth waiting for. The news was as comforting to me as a friendly hand on the shoulder.

They say that the army is going to build a barracks at São Félix. And there is talk again about the Araguaia Territory. A delegate from INCRA informs me that some have proposed São Félix as the capital of the proposed Territory, since São Félix is a "hot" social issue.

Yesterday at Mass, we meditated on the parables of

mercy (The Lost Sheep, The Lost Coin, and The Prodigal Son). God is good, more than we think or believe, more than our interpretations of the Bible and of moral theology can say. God loves man with a surprisingly aware concern. God shows a certain passion for man, a passion which became Passion in Christ. One must always reopen the horizon of trust and reaffirm daily ones faith in this splendid love of God. We are too much accustomed to measure the heart of God by the narrowness of our human heart.

9/21: We received news from Serra Nova, that Alita had had a row with the "prefeito" (mayor), Valdon Varjão. It seems that he finally got an earful of truth that he was long overdue for. His only resort was the coward's way out: he relieved Alita of her job as teacher.

Yesterday we heard on the radio that Geisel is going to get together on Wednesday with four ministers and the governors of Pará, Amazonas, Goiás, Maranhão, and Mato Grosso, for an impact study on the spheres of development in Amazonia.

It seems that the region's "hour" is being hastened, and it will not go well for the "little ones."

The Synod begins on the 27th. On that same day we begin our first Diocesan Assembly, on: "Evangelization in the Modern World," and "We are the Church, the People of God." As our "starting motor" (to use the expression of a *sertanejo*), the Assembly will use the parable of the Vine and the Branches (Jn 15).

. . . Our pastoral plans will have to be provisory. The people have no room, no rights. Launched on our way by the Spirit, we must join them, in exodus, in struggle.

Mercedes has been on duty these days at the

"Leonardo Vilas Boas" center, to help Orlando, who is sick. It seems that there are two hundred and some cases of malaria to attend to there. Orlando and Sister spoke together at some length, and he manifested a desire to meet me. With all his defects and possible errors, he is a fighting man, a victim of a cause. I hope to meet him some day. [I did, in fact, meet him, not long after this. He was very effusive. We spoke at length on our common cause, and he was noble enough to tell me how he had changed his opinion about the church's mission among the Indians....]

In the office which we pompously call our 'prelazia' (chancery)—which was already under repressive surveillance—I placed a photo of a clay statue of the Virgin, offering up her Son, which Frei Fernando sent me. He says that the statue was inspired by the text of a letter I sent them when they—the three Dominicans—were in prison at Tiradentes:

> "Friend Pedro:
> A people and a woman,
> a poor woman.
> A little bit of us,
> a little bit of you,
> a little bit of the many who choose
> the struggle for justice
> as their own special way of loving.
> In her liberation
> she begets her liberator
> and returns,
> Our Lady of Liberation."

I have been paging through the Bulletin of the Holy Year, published by the Central Commission for the Holy

Year. It is number 5. It came to me *gratis,* I suppose because I'm a bishop.

I have been trying for days to reconcile myself with the "Holy Year of Reconciliation," and haven't succeeded in doing so. Paul VI is pope and his decisions, in any case, merit my respect. Nevertheless, I just can't reconcile myself with the Holy Year.

In this issue, n. 5 of the Bulletin, Jean Rodhain publishes a "Socio-statistical Prospectus on Pilgrimages during the Holy Year of 1975." In it, he attempts to persuade people to make the expensive trip, and lashes out at those who are "distressed," "simplistic" in their notions of poverty, and "indoctrinated by clever clerics." He recognizes that some object to the Holy Year "out of apostolic concerns."

I don't know what category I belong in, but I do know that after reading Rodhain's article I feel even less convinced of his apologia for the Holy Year.

Perhaps the Holy Year is only for Christians of the First and Second Worlds.

I don't believe I'm lacking either in a sense of pilgrimage, or in nostalgia for the Rock of Peter and history. I believe in Peter. And I passionately long for reconciliation. Perhaps my absence and my distance—in obscure faith and in silent prayer—are the only valid contribution I can make to the Holy Year of Reconciliation.

11/15: I am in Goiânia. Getting over an attack of malaria, which reached its painful, asphyxiating crisis on October 23, the very date of the third anniversary of my episcopal ordination.... During my illness I was visited by eight officials of the Aeronautics Department. With great deference, they had come to ask my opinion as to whether Luciara or Santa Terezinha would be a better

location for an advanced campus of the USP of São
Paulo. A curious visit. A curious request.
These weeks of fever and convalescence have been
rich in human poverty. I don't know why, but I've had a
feeling that the slowdown occasioned by this illness
somehow marks the beginning of a new stage in my life.
Be that as it may, we are always beginning, and everything is new, in God's grace. I have read more. I have
prayed more deeply. I've come out of it more...
grateful.

I'm going to São Paulo to attend the General Assembly of the National Council of Bishops.

Today, the 15th, Brazil votes for its senators and de-
puties. This is the only matter of some importance on
which Brazilians do not vote "indirectly." And this time,
because renewal groups have been more realistic, and
because the people are more aware of the issues, the
MDB (Brazilian Democratic Movement)—the only "opposition" party—has a good chance on the electoral
slate. Throughout this whole campaign, freedom has
pervaded the atmosphere, like a gust, a tiny gust, of
fresh air. At least someone has been able to say in public
that something was not going right in this giant of a
country.

The day before yesterday, here in Goiânia, I was talking to a young married woman with two small children
(a girl, three years old, with a Quechuan name, and a
boy a few months old). Her husband is outside Brazil:
one more of those Latin Americans anonymously involved in bringing about the "great revolution." We
were talking with R., and we understood each other.
Nevertheless, when got around to the "crunch" of the
"utopian" hope and poverty of the gospel—the "other"

means for saving the world—we ran into the brick wall of R.'s iron logic.

These people are admirable brothers in the passion for justice, and we can and ought to accompany them, to join them on the road. And we should do so without having to shamefacedly gloss over the gratuitous power of the faith which we Christians possess—or rather, which possesses us.

Some days ago I had a similar talk with a group of teachers and intellectuals from Minas. They are in search of an experiment in country living and in freedom for their lives, based on a Marxist option, as their response to the society of the present.

In the prelature, the people are doing what little they can, by way of resistance. The "stubbornness" of the people is a wellspring of energies for survival. Or is the instinct for survival the wellspring of the people's hard-headedness. . .?

December. In Santa Terezinha, from the 10th to the 17th, we held the second annual meeting for the entire pastoral team of the prelature. It was a whole week long, so as to provide us with study time, as well as our regular work review and planning for the next six-month period.

The letter from Edgar, who is in prison in São Paulo, was with us like a watchword.

We reflected on the theology of liberation in the context of a particular church: in this case, our own little church of São Félix, here and now. We defined what we mean by "living the faith," and by communing in and communicating this Christian faith, in a context of the gospel, history, and reality. We as a group feel the prob-

lem, common to all Latin America, of popular religious
attitudes—the sustenance, the amulet, the alignment,
and the life: all of these at once, mixed together in deli-
cate promiscuity. Because of the concrete circumstances
which persecution has created all about us, we feel called
to be, modestly but faithfully, a small "frontier" church:
someone is able to dialogue with Christ through the
medium of us. Our hope is a call and a light for many
generous souls who "fight alongside us, without realizing that this struggle is, in Christ, salvation." We pray
intensely. At certain times we have been overwhelmed
by the feeling that our people have been trapped in a
dead-end street. And this same feeling has returned us,
like an ocean swell, to him who is our Rock, in whose
glorified hands, forever, are the already liberated ways
of man. . . . The closing eucharist was worthy of the Acts
of the Apostles: the Lord was present in our midst. We
must go on believing, in an attitude of total availability.

On our return trip (two days on boat along the
Araguaia), the team-community, different in so many
ways—sex, vocations, abilities—kept breaking into song,
dialogue, and jokes, with all the comforting cohesiveness
of a big apostolic family.

12/25: At any rate it is Christmas. An authentic Christmas, because it is poverty and good will for redemption
and an unquenchable desire to build justice into true
PEACE. Christ, the Son of God, is the son of Mary, a
member of our human people.

12/29: There is no way to write this asthmatic diary of
mine with any continuity.

I have just finished reading (late as usual) a synthesis of Raimondo Panikkar's *Conversaciones en Madrid:* Spanish intellectualism (or, at least, Spanish notoriety), between skepticism and dogmatism, rather outspoken in its freedom of expression—although it is a bit formal and bourgeois, this liberty, perhaps rather distant from the people—with a good contribution from Joaquín Ruiz Jiménez.

Just today a young married couple, plain tourists (he, an engineer of the São Paulo Metro; she, a student), were asking me about, among other things ecclesiastical and civil, the Opus Dei, the cursillo movement, the future of Spain. . . .

They were just two more of the already many young people who have come to visit us, drawn by the same wavelength of restlessness and choice, beckoned by the little light of this *sertanejo* candle, which is the church of São Félix.

Here and there in "civilization," the young in years and the young in heart are accompanying us. Sometimes I think that our mission—the special "charism" of our church (it does have its charism, doesn't it?)—may consist, both here and there in a sort of long-distance witness. The roads of God intercross. And grace has its multiple intercommunicating vessels. Sometimes I make a review of these seven years in Mato Grosso, and of the motives, conscious or unconscious—providential, in any case—that brought me here and keep me here. And I feel that in the church, in humanity saved by Christ, there are no distances or gaps. We all live and are and do in every place, in all places at once. The communion of saints is a fact.

I mentioned that youth accompanies us. Among the young people of today, the "ideal" of justice has its good adherents. But so does the "ideal" of the flight into drugs; so does the "ideal" of the sex instinct; so does the "ideal" of the sweet, fast life of latest model cars; so does the "ideal" of crass greed, which dreams of finishing well at a good school, thus insuring a high-paying profession and a lucrative future.

1975. 2/23: The cataract has grown and my vision is blurred. My liver has become as touchy as a retired grandparent. I have celebrated the forty-seventh anniversary of my, let us say, existence. My beard, which is white when I let it grow, gives me away. I get tired easily. Fr. Viñas, that suave, sensible man from Vich, used to say that setbacks begin after forty.

Both my temperament and my responsibilities cause me frequent anxieties. I feel the nearness of misery, of a society from which there seems to be no way out, and of death. I have a sense of the skin-deep decrepitude of human life. . . . (I believe that I can empathize with what the stubborn and faithful Padre Llanos—whose impenitent youth has shaken so many for a third of a century—calls sometimes age, sometimes Christian pessimism.) I also have a greater awareness of faith, a nearer, realer, simpler and more final experience of hope. I believe, "know," that we shall rise again and that the world is traveling imperturbably towards its glorification. It is no longer possible for me to cease believing in this.

. . . Today, to the desolate accompaniment of her mother's cries, a little Gorotiri Indian girl, from the forests of Pará, died. There was no remedy for her in the Indian Hospital. She died of a massive case of worms. Sister Mercedes, whom I regard as a sort of delegate presence in the indigenous world that surrounds us, has attended to both mother and child with the utmost delicacy. And now, at three in the afternoon, beneath the gaze of a between-rains, Sunday sun, Mercedes is traveling to Gorotiri, with the disconsolate mother and her dead child. Far from her people and their funeral rites, the poor woman felt the loss of death all the more deeply, as she beat her breast and her whole body, in rhythm with the sorrow of her people. . . .

And here ends, for the moment, the diary in which I have been haltingly pouring myself out, since the first month of August when I came to live in Mato Grosso.

20

In the mission, in the prelature, life—this life that goes on giving meaning to my credo—has become calm and withdrawn, like some crouching wild beast of the *sertão*.

"Official" repression (there is also an "officious," meddlesome repression throughout the country, which the government invokes under the justifying label of "parallel power") has changed its game and its tactics. No longer interested in provoking scandal, it would like to dialogue (above all, with the church, which it wants as an ally in the confrontation of its own contradictory inner forces). And so the government offers its handshake, bridles its tongue and . . . goes its own way as usual.

This diplomatic norm has been adopted "at the top" of

government, mainly (it is believed) through the artful sponsorship of its *"éminence grise,"* General Couto de Golbery.

The image of Brazil that the government has tried to project has always been more centered on the "Revolution" (which put the present form of government in power), than on the people of Brazil. And good relations with the church form an indispensable part of this "good image."

In all fairness, it must be said that not all bishops (to mention those of my "class") think this way. Enough of them believe in the good intentions of Geisel's government. My opinion, for what it's worth, is that neither Geisel nor his government nor this régime gives the orders. The "system" is prior and superior to them, and the system gives the orders: the designedly capitalistic, diabolically multinational, and strategically "Latin American" system.

Some, bishops or otherwise (too many, at any rate), believe in a dialogue at the upper echelons. I'm not a specialist in church history, but my nose tells me that this sort of dialogue has been going on for centuries, with the best of intentions, and with the same results as we can all see here. I distrust it, because it seems neither democratic nor ecclesial to me, and hence, it does not seem the sort of dialogue that I can enter into honestly. We have engaged in centuries of concordats and agreements with power, at the expense of the poor, whether or not Constantine was the prototype of them all.

What is certain is that, within the scope of its input, Geisel's government is making a review of its projects. For that very reason, we are in a moment of pause, of looking forward to what is to come. Looking at what hits us closest to home, Geisel's government has created *"Poloamazonia"*:

fifteen poles or spheres of development for the entire region of Legal Amazonia. This project can draw on a fabu-
lous reserve of *cruzeiros* and subsidiary undertakings, basically aimed at beefing up the cattle-raising and mining
industries. One of its main objects will be the industrializa-
tion of farming (in accord with the policies of Agriculture
Minister Paulinelli), which will give the greatest opportunity to powerful interests within the country and to multinational corporations. More recently (superimposed as a
partial corrective), a *"Polo-centro"* for the various spheres
has been created.

The history of the regime's paternalistic "impact
studies" is strewn with bitter lessons. The "Revolution" has
backed now this, now that project (such as the Transamazon) which, with other grandiose plans, have come to nothing. All of this inclines one to be rather cautious.

One thing is sure: the small farmers of the region—our
posseiros—without resources and without recourse, will
have to yield, will have to leave. Within "Poloamazonia,"
we are "Pole #1," exclusively dedicated to cattle raising.
The *peones,* moreover, are simply passing from a state of
slavery to the great *fazendas,* to one of forced unemploy-
ment. Clearing, burning, planting forage—all is being
mechanized, so that human workhands are becoming superfluous. On top of this, there is the well-known second
phase of layoffs on these great cattle-raising estates, once
they have made their initial penetration and settled in with
their cattle. The Indians are being inexorably fenced off
by highways, *fazendas,* and mining enterprises. Recent
Ministers of the Interior have nauseatingly repeated the
permanent thesis of the "Revolutionary Regime," vis à vis
the indigenous population: let them be integrated into the
"national community" as soon as possible, and become

"productive" persons, so as not to form an obstacle to the developmentalist progress of the country. The greatest *"sertanistas"* in the country—specialists in contact with the Indians—have dramatically decried this whole business of "disintegrating integration." They themselves, in an historic "mea culpa," have qualified this policy as a fatal, artificial ploy, aimed at exterminating various Indian nations.

Capitalism, new or old, with or without velvet gloves, is inexorable. In its system, the little people only count to the extent that they serve as anonymous cogs in the gears of the almighty machine.

And not just the little people, but the middling and the not-so-great, as well! Recently an ex-director of a *fazenda* told me: "Only the very great count, today." "And," he added, "the multinationals."

If I'm not a specialist in church history, still less am I a specialist in political economy. So I'll be silent and let time speak for itself.

*   *   *

I have been speaking of "the life that has given meaning to my credo," and, after this long ramble of shared experiences and of pages from my diary, I have finally come to the end of it, thus far.

I continue working as a bishop in this world-farm of northern Mato Grosso. Facing the plans and programs of power, the pastoral team of this prelature—bishop, priests, nuns, and laity—striving to be faithful to the basic option we cannot abandon, are spread out in small, "mixed" communities in our various *patrimonios,* performing a work of informal education and medical aid, outside the official channels. Ours is a work of global and contemporary consciousness raising, of particular or generalized evangelization, of the pastoral administration of the sacraments, of eucharistic celebrations geared to the life of the people, and of the slow and patient formation of small communities, without neglecting the shapeless mass of the majority.... The gospel is a hidden leaven, a tenacious seed that lies buried. It is so here, too, in this tiny, infinite, scarred yet stubborn prelature of northwestern Mato Grosso, in the vaunted Legal Amazonia, in the heart of hearts of Brazil....

II

The God and Father
Of Our Lord Jesus Christ

1

The first feeling I had about God, was that he was a really unique being and that he really counted. He counted in the life of my parents, in the life of my family. God was a name, a threat, a goal, a consolation, and a constant, last resort.

The ones who counted with God were the good; those who did not count with God were the bad. The few times I heard anyone referred to as an atheist, I could tell he was some sort of degenerate. (Nevertheless, I discovered that there were some nonpracticing Catholics in our small town of Balsareny and, although atheists and nonpracticing Catholics should theoretically have been lumped together, some of these nonpractitioners were good people and even, as in the case of Liborio, the neighboring tailor, good friends of the family.)

God counted in the life of my people. The calendar revolved about him. They said that he counted in the life of the whole country and the world. He did everything, saw everything, judged everything: everything depended on him.

Pagans who lived in distant, backward parts of the earth, were those savages whom the missionaries sought out and were sometimes killed by. Such as Blessed Almató, our fellow countryman.

146

When I was two years old, I was sent to the school of the Dominican Sisters of the Annunciation, which was located across the street from our house, on the other side of the plaza and of the sun. And both at home and in school I was taught how to say my morning and night prayers. We used to pray the family rosary, while I, near the stove, was nearly always a little hazy and half-asleep. We infallibly attended Mass, of course. I don't remember much more than this. I do remember quite well, however, the Novenas for the Poor Souls that we attended, where I held on to my father's hand and where I woke fitfully and fearfully before the immense canvas depicting the souls in flames.

After the war—and also, as an amateur, at clandestine Masses in my uncles' country houses, during the war—I was an altar boy; as were my brother and cousins, in a sort of Levitical continuity. And as an altar boy, I began to acquire a familiarity with the things of God, with the priests, the sacraments, with death and the life to come. On the one hand, this familiarity did a bit to demythologize religion for me. (Every oldtime altar boy became a candidate either for the priesthood or for anticlericalism.) Mossén Pere (Father Pedro), the pastor used to smoke in the sacristy, vested, and sometimes past the scheduled hour for the beginning of Mass. The priests used to have their little quarrels, their foibles. They used to count the collections a bit too eagerly. On the other hand, this familiarity put me on the inside of religion and made it something that was mine, an inalienable right.

For my First Communion, I literally knew my whole catechism by heart, with all the assurance of an apologete.

The war, without priests, without religious services in our shadowy Romanesque church which had been desecrated by fire, and with the onset of my premature puberty, introduced me to a new "religion" of personal, conflict-ridden prayer: as I was pestered by my childish sins, I would pray to God, discussing them with him and asking him to be understanding.

The war also showed me something of the heroic side of religion. So many priests, religious, and "good Catholics" died for their religion, as did my priestly uncle, Luis. And so many lived by it, in hiding and in many risky situations, like Fr. Bertrans and other priests I knew, sweating and anonymous, saying all those farmhouse, dresser-top Masses, without liturgical vestments or ornaments.

The remarks of my elders and my own observations soon led me to distinguish between the right-wing and religion, between being Catholic and living the faith. In the Catholic Youth "Local," this distinction would become all the clearer to me. It was one thing to make ardent protestations of being a Catholic, for example, and quite another "to live a life of grace." Being a Catholic, I sometimes thought, was like belonging to a party of some sort. Add to this that mothers, aunts, and grandmothers were all most ardent Catholics. So were—without discussion—children and old people. . . .

After the war, with the arrival of the Nationalists, once the initial stage of euphoria had passed, it began to seem to me as if religion had been used. From a distance, from the catacombs of our pine-covered hills, via the "underground" radio, or behind the closed shutters of my house, the Nationalists were looked upon as crusaders, as soldiers of Christ the King—as I was later to learn. They were the "liberation" that had been coming to us slowly, like a longed-for gift of God. But then there were the troops, mercenaries or simple recruits, whose eyes devoured the women standing in line as they passed on parade. There were the Moors, pulling out gold fillings from dead men's teeth. There was the chaplain who was enraged that some-one from town had covered over the fire-damaged main altar with a red cloth. And there was the unholy alliance between those who were formerly leftists, now joining the Falange. The Nationalists, then, no longer seemed to me to represent "religion," saved and defended. Religion was something mixed and impure, and you had to distinguish between the cross and the sword.

Then the priests came back, and I went to school with the Mossén (Mossén is the title by which Catalans ordinar-ily call their priests). I was an altar boy, officially. In those days, I already felt frequent pious fervors: at services, heavy with incense, before the Blessed Sacrament ex-posed, and at Sunday Mass; in the hymns we sang, most of which were still from Verdaguer or from Mossén Romeu, while some were from the still somewhat esoteric repertory of Gregorian Chant; in the great solemn feasts of the year: Christmas, above all, Holy Week, the Month of August of the Mother of God, Corpus Christi, and the Immaculate Conception. Sunday services (*"funcions,"* as we called them) I sometimes felt fatally dull; at other times I lived them with an initial "predestined" devotion. . . . My confes-sions, my repeated confessions, kept me in the balance of a fidelity which I never reneged on. My scruples, which I later brought to the seminary with me, and which were yet to live a long life within me, were really the equivalent of a tormented profession of faith in the "true" religion. At any rate, the most important thing for me as a child and as a young lad, was always to come back to the grace of God.

I was prematurely an *"avanguardista."* After the war I joined the "Catholic Action," even if it did seem a bit Casti-lian, a bit imported. At that time, the slogans, the *teatro católico,* the study circles for my elders, the publications, the excursions, the "caramelles" (something like caroling groups, only at Easter), and the activities at our parish center—all of these were my life, my obsession. Religion, church, faith, all rolled into one, without dividing lines, in my feelings. God was all of these things for me. How could it have been otherwise?

2

Once I was in the seminary—the minor seminary and the novitiate—I espoused the cause of safeguarding the one thing necessary, namely, grace. And I became deeply pious, especially in the novitiate, with all its meticulous fidelity. So much so that, at that time, I literally "sensed" the presence of God which, protected by eyes that were always cast down, became my very lifebreath, a sort of second pulse. I spent all my siestas (which were not, by the way, spent in bed, but sitting upright at an austere desk) praying before the tabernacle. The good Brother Riera, who was so fond of the *"blanca Mare de Déu de la Mercé"*— the statue of Our Lady of Mercy, at Vich, would often surprise me as I knelt there.

My enthusiasm was aroused by the Lives of the Saints which we used to read in the refectory during the novitiate: St. Francis Xavier, who was later to become *"El Divino Impaciente"*—the divine, impatient man—of my seminary soirées, and the spur of my missionary ambitions; St. Peter Claver, whose mosquitoes I have met, quite alive, here in Mato Grosso; Saint Therese of the Child Jesus, above all, who became, from that time on, my life-companion.

The Story of a Soul became *the* book of my novitiate. Providentially. Because in it, I made some marvelous discoveries for my faith: that God is our Father; that he is more, even, than a mother who cannot forget the children of her womb; that he has us "tatooed" on his arm; that the kingdom of heaven is reserved for children; that God is love; that the prayer of Christians is the Our Father; that Christ left us, as his last will and testament, the New Commandment of love; that the neighbor is something essential and central to Christian faith; that a disciple of Jesus owes himself to his brothers; that he must offer and spend his life for them; that the most hidden contemplative nun could and should become a universal missionary. . . .

The Story of a Soul also opened up the Bible to me. Isaiah and John came to me via the hand of the little Carmelite of Lisieux.

The repeated Spiritual Exercises we made, especially those following Fr. Casanovas' serious, well-reasoned treatises, established me in the conviction that God is the principle and end of our Life (as I would later write: "Tú mi Principio y mi fin./ Yo un ahora peregrino / de Ti a Ti."—"Thou, my principle and my end./ I, a now-pilgrim/ from Thee to Thee.") Besides being a goal, eternity came to be the value, the constant reason for my existence. "Quid hoc ad aeternitatem?" This world was indeed "but a shadow that passes."

On another level, the liturgy bathed that discarnate, Ignatian background (which has remained to this day the trusty backbone of my spirit) with light, with powerful spiritual emotions, and even with an imperturbable joy. During my seminary training, I lived the great celebrations of the liturgical year with special intensity: Christmas, Holy Week, Pentecost, All Saints. From this period on, I celebrated Easter with a poetic passion and with all those insights we glimpse in real faith. I had discovered Easter;

and I believe that this was the greatest discovery in all my spiritual life: the cornerstone of my hope in the resurrection—Christ's and ours—which today channels and expresses the total content of my Christian faith.

Schulzter, Guardini, Odo Cassel—the sober evocations of Gregorian Chant—the music of Palestrina and Vittoria, of Gelineau and, later, Deiss—all of these constituted an amalgam of art and prayer, a "sacrament" of meditation and committed living quite attuned to my bent. Every person has the right to live his own, personal liturgy. This by no means detracts from my recognition of the liturgy's essential function in creating community. But the Word is made flesh in the concrete terrain of each human person. God speaks his Word in the dialect of each individual.

One thing I owe to a rigid teacher from the days of my philosophical studies, when all the exterior scaffolding of my novitiate was falling in pieces about me: he introduced me to Saint Paul. The encounter may have been somewhat fanatical—since we all used to be able to rattle off the epistles in Latin (and a few of the more courageous of us, in Greek)—but I indeed encountered St. Paul. And through him, the Bible as a whole, with its overarching themes of the mystery of Christ and salvation history.

3

Summing up my attitude toward the Bible, I can say that, in the measure that I have grown in knowing it through meditation and reading (not through any great, specialized studies, I must admit), I have grown more and more convinced, whether by new or old exegetical standards, that the surest and most salutary reading (and I mean "salutary" in the sense of salvation by God in Jesus

Christ) is the humble and faith-filled reading that absorbs the scriptures, either in deep drafts or tiny sips, in the light of:

—"key" names
—peak moments in the history of Israel
—the great "wonders" God has worked in his people and in his Christ
—the "commonplaces" of consolation and hope
—the paradigmatic sayings of the Lord
—the major lines of the confession of faith of the apostles and the first Christian communities.

My experience of certain fanatical, pentecostal Protestant groups, as well as of certain educational, doctrinal, and pastoral aberrations among Catholics—all of them allegedly based on the Word of God, but really based on a bad reading of that Word—has brought me to the personal and liberating conviction that the "letter (the letter of the Bible) kills," and that only "the Spirit (which is latent in the Bible) quickens." In other words: that the Word of God is greater than the Bible; that God's revelation doesn't exactly end with John; that the Word of God cannot be the privileged ghetto of certain learned men; that Jesus Christ "surpasses" himself, outside the gospel, beyond the Gospel, in the church which is his Body and in redeemed humanity, which is his fullness; that the gospel is a dynamic force of God and not a moment-monument to be visited by nostalgia-seekers and savants.

As I was thinking about what I could do to organize my errant memories for this credo that I have lived, I crammed nine typed pages with the biblical references that have most substantially nourished my faith. Mercifully,

I'm not going to transcribe all of them here; but I do want to list some, since without them my journey in faith, and the motives behind that journey, would remain unexplained:

The God of Genesis, who makes man in his image, an "approachable" God who walks through the paradise he created, who declares that everything he created is good. The interest God takes in reopening the dialogue with man who has sinned by an abuse of creation and of his lordly will and who, having sinned, "hides" himself from the eyes of God, the friendly and fulfilling Presence.

Abraham, my first saint, in chronological order. His fidelity and his "exodus" in faith (Gen 12:1 . . .). The promises, the Covenant (Gen 15 and 17).

The mission of Moses, the liberator (Ex 3), and his heart-to-heart talks with the living God (Nm 11). The great Exodus of the people, the crossing of the Red Sea, the desert, the Promised Land (Dt 8).

Gideon, such an expeditious man, a minor leader whose resources were poor, but whose confidence was great (Jg 6 and 7). Sometimes I tell Dom Helder and other bishop friends, that we must rely on "Gideonic minorities," just as much as we rely on the "Abrahamic minority."

(I should remark, parenthetically, that there were a lot of things in the Bible that frequently "rubbed" my faith, such as Israel's "privileges" vis à vis the rest of the world, that particularism as "his" people; also the brutalities and scandals of the patriarchs, prophets, and kings; and also the behavior of a God who chastises, kills, and even wipes out whole enemy populations. But this was before I achieved a simple, realistic, and global view of the Book, which is as divine as it is human.

I might also add, parenthetically, that my contact with the Bible strongly resonated with my poetic side. More than once I compared my reading of the Bible with that of Rubén Darío, and even, Renan; without any ulterior, iconoclastic intentions, of course.)

Samuel and Yahweh's call (1 Sm 3), in a situation where the priests themselves were prostituting the temple, was the prototype of a vocation that is responded to.

David, the chosenness of his youth, his sin and his repentance; his "heart after the heart of God," despite all his regrets; the covenant God made with his House; and then, "the Son of David."

The Maccabees, as a heroic family of martyrs.

Job and the mystery of human suffering, the hard trust in the Lord which challenges the impious, the sense of death and that "blind" hope that one will see "with these eyes."

The Psalms, as an echo and translation of ones own spirit. The force of destiny, sin, human anguish, and hope in the presence of God, the Rock. . . . Prayer and poetry blended, to become the song of a whole people. . . . One Wednesday night in Sabadell, Psalm 41 came to me as a confirmation to my option for the poor and needy: "Happy is he who has regard for the lowly and the poor!" There were so many others: the "thirsting for God" (63); the pilgrimage song (84); the goodness of the God who "is love" (103); the pilgrim's greeting to Jerusalem: "How I rejoiced when they told me . . . (122); the "De Profundis" (130); "For his love is everlasting" (136); the exile's ballad (137); "Yahweh, you have probed me and know me" (139)....

The prophets, as men who are "called," to announce and denounce. Awakeners of the people. Men who have met the living, awesome God. Men compelled irresistibly by the Word ("It is Yahweh who speaks! Who, then, will not prophesy?"). Living, scandalous "signs" of the Word of God. Watchtowers over the whole wide world, even to the days to come of the Messiah. Their wrath. Their fidelity under persecution. Their courage in the face of the great. Their martyrdom. Their "love for the brethren" (Jeremiah). Their crying out for justice (Amos . . .).

Isaiah: for whom I feel the deepest admiration. A marvelous poet, the "Fifth Evangelist." "The Book of the Consolation of Israel" is one of my favorite "places" in the Bible.

My first reading of the gospels was loving, detailed, and coloristic. With a nostalgic faith in the friend. Everything about him interested me. I was a passionate reader of the great lives of Jesus and of biblical commentaries (Grandmaison, Lagrange, Ricciotti, William, the Bible of Montserrat, the Jerusalem Bible . . .).

Later, I came to think of them more as the good news, the joyful news, news from God of what he had to tell us and did tell us through Jesus Christ.

Points I would underline in the gospels:

—The Prologue to John: the subsistent Word, through whom all things were made, the Word who set up his tent among us, and whose glory "we have seen."

—The Annunciation to Mary and the Magnificat (Lk 1).

—Joseph: his dark faith, his generous fidelity (Mt 1).

—Bethlehem: the Nativity in poverty, on the margin, the fringes of society; the invitation to the shepherds, themselves marginal people (Lk 2); the risk-taking faith of the Magi (Mt 2).

—John the Baptizer: somber, powerful, loyal to the point of martyrdom (Jn 1: Mt 4).

—The first missionary announcement of Jesus, his rallying call (I remember the scene in Pasolini's film quite clearly!) (Mt 4). The call of the first disciples (Lk 5; Mk 1:19–20).

—The penitent woman (Lk 7), Zacchaeus (Lk 19), the faith of the woman with an issue of blood (Mk 5), Nicodemus (Jn 3), the Samaritan woman (Jn 4), the faith of the Canaanite woman (Mt 15), the confession of Peter (Mt 16), the call of Levi (Mk 2), the cure of the man born blind (Jn 9), Lazarus, Martha, and Mary (Jn 11).

—The beatitudes and the entire Sermon on the Mount, which "spiritualize" the Law and make it "new" and "radical," demanding a total life-commitment, upsetting the value of "values," the Magna Carta of the New Man: "Seek first the Reign of God. . . ." "Do not be concerned. . . ." "You cannot serve two masters . . ." etc. (Mt 5; Lk 12).

—The sign: "The Spirit of the Lord is upon me" (Lk 4); "The Good News is announced to the poor . . ." (Lk 7).

—The two "contradictory" sayings: "Whoever is not with me is against me" (Lk 11); "Whoever is not against us is with us" (Mk 9).

—"Whoever loves father or mother . . . more than me" (Mt 10).

—"Blest are your eyes because they see" (Mt 13), "Abraham rejoiced that he might see my day" (Jn 8).

—The mustard seed, the pearl of great price, the net (Mt

13): because the Kingdom is small and buried and tenacious and demanding and total.

—"Do not provide yourselves with traveling bag . . ."; "You will be hated by all on account of me . . ."; "I am sending you out like sheep among wolves" (Mt 10; Lk 9–10).

—The discourse on the Bread of Life (Jn 6): belief in it; eating his flesh; "Lord, to whom should we go? You alone have the words of everlasting life."

—"This people honors me with its lips" (Is 29; Mk 7; Mt 15).

—"If anyone wishes to follow me, he must deny his very self" (Mt 16); "Whoever puts his hand to the plough but keeps looking back . . ." (Lk 9).

—"If you do not become like little children . . ." (Mt 18).

—"Wherever two or three are gathered in my name . . ." (Mt 18).

—"I thank you, Father, for having hid these things . . ." (Mt 11).

—"Come to me, all you who labor and are heavy burdened . . ." (Mt 11).

—The Good Samaritan (Lk 10).

—The Our Father. "Ask and you shall receive" (Lk 11).

—If anyone thirsts, let him come to me and drink" (Jn 7).

—"I am the Light of the World," "Whoever keeps my word," "If the Son sets you free, you will indeed be free." (Jn 8).

—The Good Shepherd (Jn 10).

—"If you would be perfect, go sell what you have" (Mk 10).

—"It is easier for a camel to pass through the eye of a needle" (Mk 10).

—"Everyone who abandons house or brethren" (Mt 19).

—"Everyone who is ashamed of me" (Lk 12).

—"Have your loins girded" (Lk 12).

—"If you had faith the size of a mustard seed" (Lk 17).

—"Can you drink of the cup.. ?" (Mk 10).

—Jesus weeping over Jerusalem: "How often have I longed to gather your children..." (Mt 23).

—"Unless the grain of wheat falls into the ground and dies... and I, when I am lifted up..." (Jn 12).

—"The stone which the builders rejected has become the main cornerstone" (Mk 21).

—"Have you never read: I am the God of Abraham.... He is not a God of the dead" (Mt 22).

—"Heaven and earth will pass away, but my words will never pass away" (Mk 13).

—"With desire have I desired to eat this Passover with you.... Here am I among you as one who serves. You have stayed by me..." (Lk 22).

—The Parables of Mercy: the lost sheep, the prodigal son (Lk 15).

—The Last Judgment: Key to the judgment—"I was hungry... I was in prison... and you did not..." (Mt 25).

—The entire Discourse-Testament of Jesus at the Last Supper (Jn).

—Gethsemani.

—The judgment before Pilate.

—The attitude of the divine in the presence of Herod.

—The seven last, human words....

—The resurrection of Jesus, which has undergone a number of metamorphoses in me, passing from a dazzling and exultant sort of faith—a bit poetic, a bit contemplative, a bit apologetic—and from a more critical but never carping faith, to a simple and solid faith that sustains me and holds my allegiance beyond—God help me—any doubt or any possible new exegesis, a faith that harmonizes well with the new theology of the resurrection, of our resurrection. I believe that my Lord Jesus Christ lives, and that he is the life and the resurrection of men and of the world!

I underline all the texts on the resurrection and the appearances of the Risen Lord, one by one.

I felt a particular attraction to the Acts of the Apostles, ever since I became involved in the cursillo movement. Nevertheless, Pentecost, the great biblical-ecclesial fact, the liturgical solemnity, the interiorization of the Holy Spirit—all of these were a vital reference-point for my faith at a much earlier date. The first Christian community, whose attitudes are now classed as being characteristic of "neophytes, converts," continues to be a lesson and a stimulus to me.

I would also have to underline the persecution of the apostles, their integrity, and the capture and martyrdom of Stephen (Acts 4, 5, 6, 7).

Paul has often been a stimulus to me as the "man who has given his life to the cause of Our Lord Jesus Christ" (Acts 15:26). His lightning-like, radical conversion stirs my enthusiasm. Nevertheless, I have learned to distinguish in Paul what is his gospel from what is the residue of Judaism, temperament or idiosyncrasies of the man or his times.

I underline the greetings and closings of his letters, since they are so charged with human friendship and fraternal communion.

Romans: Justification by faith (4), baptism (6), the Christian "free" from sin and from the Law (6 and 7), the law of the Spirit which frees (8), "You have not received a spirit

of slavery"—creation freed (8), faith, a gratuitous gift
(9), children of the light, "it is time for you to wake from
sleep (13).

1 Corinthians: "We preach Christ crucified, a scandal..."
(1:23).... Few of you are wise or powerful... "Yet God
has chosen what the world counts as foolish.... I came
before you weak..." (1 and 2). "The time is short...
those who make use of the world as though they were
not using it..." (7). "I have made myself all things to all
men" (9). The Lord's Supper (11). The supremacy of
charity: "Though I speak with the tongues of men and
angels..." (13). The resurrection of Christ and of the
dead: "When this corruptible frame takes on incorrup-
tibility..." (15).

2 Corinthians: "The earthly tent is destroyed"... and future glory (5 and also 4). "If anyone is in Christ, he is a
new creation... now all is new!" (5).

Galatians: The reproach to Peter: "If you who are a Jew are
living according to Gentile ways" (2:14). "The life I live
now is not my own; Christ is living in me... who loved
me and gave himself up for me" (2:20). The divine son-
ship: "When the designated time had come... the spirit
of his Son which cries out in our hearts..." (4). Christian freedom: "It was for liberty that Christ freed us" (5).
"As for me, may I never boast in anything except the
cross.... All that matters is that one is created anew"
(6:14 f.).

Ephesians: A beloved text. A beautiful synthesis on the mystery of salvation and the church. "Praised be the God
and Father..." (1:3 ff.). Realized eschatology (2). Reconciliation of the "two peoples" (2:14—"It is he who is
our peace."). The New Man (2:15 and 4:13, 23 f.).

Philippians: The attitude of Christ... who emptied himself

(2). "We have our citizenship in heaven.... He will give a new form to this lowly body of ours" (3:20 f.).

Colossians: The primacy of Christ: "He is the image of the invisible God.... It pleased God to make absolute fullness reside in him.... In Christ the fullness of deity resides in bodily form" (1 and 2). "Since you have been raised up in company with Christ... put on the New Man.... There is neither Greek nor Jew here..." (3:1,9 ff.).

1 Thessalonians: "Who, after all, if not you, will be our hope or joy, or the crown we exult in...?" (2:19). The dead, at the Coming of Christ: "like those who have no hope" (4:13). "Although we could have insisted on our authority..." (2:7).

2 Thessalonians: "May our Lord Jesus Christ himself, may God our Father who loved us and in his mercy gave us eternal consolation and hope..." (2:16).

1 Timothy: "This explains why we work and struggle as we do; our hopes are fixed on the living God who is the savior of all men, but especially of those who believe" (4:10).

2 Timothy: The letter of the bishop, of the man consecrated to the gospel and to the service of his brothers and sisters. "Stir into flame the gift of God..." (1). "Remember that Jesus Christ... was raised from the dead.... If we have died with him... He is faithful..." (2). "I charge you to preach the word, to stay with this task"... (4). "A crown of righteousness... for all who have set their hearts on his coming appearance" (4:8).

Titus: "The grace of God has appeared, offering salvation to all men" (2:11).

Hebrews: "In times past, God spoke in fragmentary ways... in this, the final age he has spoken to us through his Son... heir of all things..." (1). "That by his death he might... free those who through fear of death had been slaves" (2:14 ff.). "A high priest who can... sympathize with our weakness... for he himself is beset by weakness" (4:15–5:2). The priesthood of Christ, in his blood, the New Covenant (9). The faith of the ancients, the example of Christ (11 and 12). "Let us go to him outside the camp, bearing the insult which he bore. For we have here no lasting city; we are seeking one which is to come" (13).

James: "Your faith... must not allow of favoritism" (2:1 ff.). Warnings to the rich (4 and 5).

1 Peter: "Praised be the God and Father... who in his great mercy gave us new birth" (1). Under persecution, "be ever ready to give a reason for this faith of yours" (3). Advice to the elders: "Watch over the flock... not for shameful profit" (5:1 f.). "Stay sober and alert" (5:8).

1 John: The whole letter, line by line, with passionate devotion, read an infinite number of times: Walking in the light, charity; keeping oneself from the world and from antichrists, and remaining in the truth; living like children of God: "See what love the Father has bestowed on us..." (3:1 ff.). "We have crossed over from life to death; this we know, because we love the brothers..." (3:14 f.). "My children, love must not be a matter of words or talk..." (3:18 ff.). "For *God is love... We love because he loved us first*" (4:8 ff.).

Revelation: The book of the great consolation. A passionately engaging book, which one discovers through references, little by little; which one reads, later, with the enjoyment of an initiate; whose "major" texts comfort, commit, and fulfill. Nourishment of hope amid fear, doubt, sorrow, and the seduction of life. Key to history. Vademecum of the pilgrim church, the persecuted church.

Its closing thought should be the church's constant sigh, because it is the greatest cry of our faith, the ultimate word of hope: "Amen! Come, Lord Jesus!"

4

I studied theology, of course, and Sacred Scripture, and all the other ecclesiastical "disciplines." And I had to study the whole code of canon law, since the Claretian congregation was a glorious school for canonists! (Canon law has never—I say this in all respect—"set well" with me, and it costs me some trouble even now to "take seriously" the new code that is in preparation.)

The times were not very propitious for studies. Still, we had a few bright professors who opened up new paths for us which we have traveled since, growing steadily in the freedom of faith. I would even say that, despite some of the hardships it involved, I am grateful for the Thomistic foundations on which we were so "orthodoxly" placed.

Certain important names in theology and spirituality have been real milestones along my way: Karl Adam, Schmaus, Guardini, Congar, Journet, Chenu, Häring, Voillaume, Rahner, Schillebeeckx and later, various friends and Spanish companions, such as José María González Ruiz and Fernando Sebastián, for example. These and other "classic" works are real springs from which I have drunk. Perhaps the last master-book for me (others have since been companion-books), was Durrwell's *The Resurrection of Jesus, Mystery of Salvation.*

I had a Trinitarian phase. And other phases of a faith

that was vivisected into separate articles. Since then, I have begun to cut myself off from certain theological themes that are beset with cultural appendages—philosophical categories, historical conditionings—such as that of faith. I have kept on, almost instinctively, by my readings and also, doubtless, by grace, winnowing the relative from the absolute (and who knows which is which in this relative world?), in the Bible and in tradition. Even though the process has been a timid one, it has liberated me to an extraordinary degree. As Juan Ramón Fernández experienced a progressive denudation in poetry, so have I, in faith. I believe in the "sensus fidei," by experience, let us say.

Alongside the God of the Bible, the Maker, the Most High, the Father, the God and Father of our Lord Jesus Christ, I have also had a good deal of contact in the ministry, with God the oppressor and the implacable, who sets moral and psychological conditions, who chastises, who denies recourse, who finally gets his due, who sends illness, unexplainable misfortune and death. This has been an impressive and bitter experience for me, from my earliest days as a confessor at Sabadell, up to the conversations and spontaneous expressions that form the lifelong usage of the people in this prelature. A few days ago, old Raimundo, the father of two prostitutes—one of them mute and slow-witted—turned his holy wrath on me to comment: "People like me, who don't even have a louse's skin to fall dead on, and you have the gall to say that God can't send any more 'floods'! When people 'knew better,' they used to believe that God 'changed' the weather and made the waters rise. . . ."

What is faith and adoration? What is fear and animism, in the soul of this people or any people, or in the sophisticated soul of "society," or in our own soul, often enough? I myself have felt uncomfortable before God—and artificial and conditioned and fearful. Who hasn't felt the need to believe, progressively, in a "distinct God?" Thank God that God is already "other" for me, the absolutely Other— transcendent, first and last—on the one hand; and, on the other, accessibly adorable, faithful, and friendly: the God and Father of our Lord Jesus Christ!

5

Ever since my years of seminary formation, my *prayer* was invariably either a sort of contemplative attitude— without many formulas, or with formulas that were torn from me, since I don't like praying with my mouth—or else a sort of insistent petition for myself or others—above all, for others. I have asked the Lord for a great deal. Tenaciously. And I can guarantee you that the Lord has had to get up many a night, come downstairs, and give me the loaf I was asking for. The Cursillos in Christianity only reinforced me in this prayer of supplication, with all its "*intendencia*" and its "*palancas.*" I'm not so sure that this wasn't, at times, a bit like what Jesus referred to as the "prayer of the Gentiles." What I do know, is that my intention wasn't the same as that.

Lately, I have almost left off "petitioning." I do, of course, "remind" God of certain names, certain situations. I open up my heart to him, filled with references. I place myself in his presence, powerless, and I believe that he'll take care of it.

At any rate, I have never abandoned or undervalued prayer. I believe in prayer. I often ask my friends to pray, for the prelature, for instance. I have kept an "inevitable" fidelity to prayer, and it has been a companion grace throughout all the workdays of my life. I don't care what modern psychology may have to say on the matter: I accept psychology and I believe in prayer—both at the same time. If I believe that God is present, then it seems only logical that I should "be in his presence." His presence accompanies me, and I need some "intense moments" to grasp that presence. "The spirit of prayer and prayer itself," as Vatican II taught.

Neither have I been able to get along without visits to the Blessed Sacrament. Because I believe in the real sacramental presence.

My Masses are something else, of course. The eucharist has truly become for me, the Passover of the Lord. I love the Mass. I believe that I celebrate it meaningfully. As the celebration of the sacrifice, the covenant, the encounter. As the memorial that makes him present and calls us around him. As the festive awaiting for his return. As the fraternal meal of the brethren united. As the celebration of daily life and of history, of the Passover of Jesus and the paschal mystery of man and the cosmos, loved by God, saved by God in Jesus Christ, dead and risen.

I continue to go to confession frequently. And confession liberates and strengthens me, like a bath in the reconciling blood.

I speak of *Jesus Christ* throughout these pages, as is only logical. I believe that I really believe in him! I believe in him and I adore him! I love him. I live by him and for him. I would like to give my life for him. I hope, at any rate, to die in him, in order to live with him eternally. I believe in this friend who was introduced to me by my parents, the church: God made man, born in Bethlehem, of the impoverished line of David, true son of Mary, a Jew and a worker, born of a colonialized people; a man who loved and suffered and died, persecuted and condemned by the power of men; raised up by the power of God, the man who is the Son of God, mysteriously equal to the Father, "in whom the fullness of Godhead dwells corporeally," whose Spirit animates the church; way, truth and life, savior of mankind, Lord!

My idols and vain imaginings are dead: I believe firmly, I believe only in him, the God-man who has undertaken and revolutionized and provided the solution for human history, and he is the true face of the living God and the firstborn face of the new man.

III

The Church:
People of God,
Sacrament of Salvation

1

The Catholic, apostolic, and Roman Church was, in my childhood town, the only church.

The church was the parish. The pastor, the assistants, the Dominican Sisters and the Sisters of St. Joseph. It was Sunday services (*"funcions"*). And yearly feast days. And the bishop of Vich, who confirmed me when I was two years old. And, above all, "the Holy Father," the Pope of Rome. It was also the parish "center," the Christmas plays, the Easter singing. It was the "Avanguardistes" and the "Fejocistes": and their songs, which awakened in me an intuitive ideal of a holy struggle: "O mare no ens ploreu,/ o pare no ens planyeu / si ens veieu maltractats per sectes enemigues./ Ferida en tal combat / n'es premi desitjat . . ." (O mother, do not weep for us / O father, do not cry for us / if you see us ill-treated by hostile sects. / A wound received in such a fight / is but a token of delight.)

The church was soon to become, for me, a persecuted church. The revolution of '36 broke out, and my precociously heroic child's eyes had to watch the burnings of saints and convents, the flight of Sisters and priests, the destructive raving of the anarchist militia, the blood of the martyrs: the unforgettable stains on the walls of the town cemetery, like those on the streets of Navás, in the earlier uprising of '34. I accompanied and hid persecuted religious and "Catholics." I lived with them in farmhouses, in the shadows.

As I said in the preceding chapter, the weaknesses of some Catholics whom I regarded as model Christians, because they were my "elders and betters" and then, above all, the disappointment I experienced at the behavior of the Nationalists on their reentry, provided me with a basis for a certain critical spirit in church matters. There were good and bad Catholics, then. The church should be, above all, a life: "the life of God's grace." Everyone seemed to find it too easy to call himself a Catholic. Some venerable figures, like Carlets de Cal Casas, the organist, whom I shall always remember, as well as some worthy priests, like Mosén Joan, established my image of what an ideal "man of the church" ought to be.

When I was eleven years old, I decided to become a priest. Yes, I believe that it was my decision. And from then on, the church was my life. I can honestly say that it has been so to this day, with a passion. All my rebellions and liberties have been the fruit of my identification with the church. It has pained me, and pains me, because I love it. And since I love it, I want it to be different. I can criticize it and even do it violence, because it is mine, too. As it has for many others, the church has changed from being my mother, to being my sister, my family, the family of God, a people which has already reached fulfillment in Jesus Christ, its head, but which we are all engaged in building up. This means me, too, as a priest, as a bishop. It is also that "chaste courtesan" of which the Fathers spoke, the unfaithful but ever-loved spouse, in the likeness of Israel, the mystery of the universal People of God, which is yet barely a "remnant".... I know that the church is infinitely greater than I, yet I·also know that it depends on me, and that it *is* as I am, and as I do. I know that the church is still my mother, old and beloved, doting yet gloriously alive, prior to me, the breast and milk and lap on which I depend in my new and tribulation-filled life, the cause both of my discontent and of my stubborn fidelity. I am ready to give my life for it, and I am traveling toward it, I, a sighing pilgrim, as toward the great House that will be my heritage forever.

My, I'm getting carried away!

Getting back to what I was saying: I entered the seminary of Vich, and then joined the Claretian congregation. During my student years, the "dirty laundry" of the house and the critical vision which I received from my studies, readings, and some perceptive teachers, accustomed me to a rebellious attitude. I thought, read, spoke, and wrote from a rebel's standpoint.

Then there were the intrigues and antipathies between the secular and religious clergy which I had already sensed when, at twelve years of age, I decided to "go over" to the congregation. I later witnessed these hostilities in major skirmishes between bishops and provincials, superiors and pastors, between Catholic Action and other movements and associations. The closed provincialism of each religious institute—each "superstructure within the structure of the church," as Cardinal Tabera, the late president of the Sacred Congregation of Religious, used to say. Each of these institutes seemed to ambition becoming a be-all and end-all, a sort of parallel church. The formation we received was often stifling and dehumanizing, without any appeal or recourse. The obedience that was asked of us was, besides being "blind," irritatingly irrational.

What we called religious poverty was often a lie or, at least, a pharisaical distinction between personal poverty and the collective wealth of the institute. Then there were all those timetables and regulations that hampered our apostolate, sacrificing both the inward and outward man; the abyss which gaped between our life, organization, and methods, and the helter-skelter life of the man on the street; the celibacy which many felt as a bitter form of violence and a shameful imposition; the lack of ideals and zeal which one encountered in so many religious men and priests who had made their compromises with the world, were frustrated, and felt "condemned" to be "*sacerdotes in aeternum.*" "Our things" in the congregation always seemed to be so "different" from the things of the church—so much so, that one could never see how to connect them with the things of the kingdom of God or with the pressing needs of the world of men. And what about our fossilized canon law, our unappealable magisteriums, those encyclicals and pastoral letters that were always putting someone in tow. Pastoral practice was so routine, mixed-up, or nonexistent—those joint pastoral commissions that were often just a pastoral trunk, without head or feet. All of these things which we had swallowed and spat out for so many years—no matter whose "fault" they were, diocesan or our own—all of those things that "rubbed" one in the congregation, in this or that diocese, in the church in general, and which, one intuitively sensed, could not be compatible with the will of God, the gospel of Christ, or the kingdom, had to stop. It was impossible to imagine that they wouldn't stop! We had to change a great deal, urgently, to resolve it, to change "all" of it. . . !

I was getting to be a radical.

Nevertheless, I never really contemplated leaving the congregation; and, of course, I never considered leaving the priesthood. And not even in my wildest dreams could I ever think of leaving the church. In those youthful days I always held that the "revolution" must be an "inside job." In this respect I am in sympathy with the declarations of other rebels, like Hans Küng.

2

I always liked church history and I used to enjoy reading Daniel-Rops. I experienced an intoxicating nostalgia in reflecting on the "first Christians": Lives of St. Paul (Holzner), the Acts of the Martyrs, the Fathers—Ignatius, bishop of Antioch, is another of "my" saints. I went through the evocative fever of the Middle Ages and its monks (Raymond's *Three Religious Rebels*), its society, its cathedrals, and even its crusades (which alternately scandalized and attracted me), the thoughts of Nicholas Berdyaev (!), Francis of Assisi and the Mendicants (Assisi is the town I have liked best). The counter-reformation, with its saints, theologians, and missionaries, also lifted my spirit for some time. The Spanish *siglo de oro* thrilled and filled me with its holiness and art. I even came to think that the church could hardly have asked more of it. . . .

For the eighteenth and nineteenth centuries, I felt nothing but disgust. There was, of course, Pius IX and the Immaculate Conception, and St. Pius X and the eucharist. And a few saints. But for the rest. . . .

Pius XII, in those days of his tormented and prestigious reign, was an untouchable focus of veneration: his white figure with arms outstretched in the form of a cross, his

Marian proclamations, the openness he showed, in his discourses and audiences, toward science and the new forms of human unrest. He was the focus of my ardent Roman Catholicism, of my steadfast devotion to the vicar of Christ—which was also a Claretian legacy from the staunch defender of papal infallibility at Vatican I. It was hard for me to accept the change to John XXIII, an old man with big ears, who didn't seem to be "on the inside" of anything. Yet now, I have come to love him so much, and continue to regard him as the prophet-patriarch of the new church, now free again. Then it was hard for me to accept Paul VI, because he was "no substitute" for Pope John, and because I began to be "disillusioned" by what seemed to be his balancing acts. I have since come to understand him, to criticize him, and to compassionate him, for whom I pray, with whom I am in communion, and sometimes fraternal disagreement, in the freedom of faith.

3

I have already mentioned that Vatican II was a great light in my life. It gave one a "reason" for having suffered and loved so many things. It fed so many flagging hopes. It was really a "window" opened to the wind of the Spirit and to the cries of a suffering humanity. A new springtime for the church. I drank in its documents, especially *Lumen Gentium, Gaudium et Spes* and *Ad Gentes. Lumen Gentium* still moves me.

I have since come to feel that Vatican II accomplished a great deal that is of value: through the things it intuited, the things it "let go," the doors it opened irreversibly, the Christian liberty it won for all of us in the church, for the profession of service to the world which the Council

Fathers, and through them—at least theoretically—the church, made.

Vatican II was a starting leap. But the church, too, surpasses itself, and Vatican II was not the last word. For me, and I suppose for others, the Council had the Christian merit of demythologizing the church as an institution, as a history, as the "only *locus* of salvation." By this I do not mean to say that Vatican II denied anything that the church has always said or blurted out about itself. It simply translated it. I said that it demythologized. It also did away with a lot of older adherences. It recognized the creativity of the Spirit and the freedom of the sons of God. And it had the courage, however timid, to state the "mea culpa" that the church was centuries-overdue in admitting.

Vatican II greatly encouraged the faith of the community: it was like a new, collective baptism, or, as the Council popes, John and Paul, both said, "A New Pentecost."

Starting from the ground floor up, so to speak, the Council began building on the forgotten motif of the church as the *People of God,* an entire people of the elect, a whole messianic and priestly community.

With this, the hierarchy ceased to be "the" church. And we began to feel, with a rejuvenated faith, that all of us—lay men and women, too—were the church. It would be overly optimistic to say that hierarchism, clericalism, and ecclesiastical *machismo* ended, *comme ça,* with the Council. My experience as a priest and bishop have taught me, frequently, that the contrary is the case. Even today, and in these latitudes which are much less conditioned by solemn traditions, laymen—let alone women—are "generously" tolerated. When they are admitted to an Assembly or to some post, they are not accepted as equals. They can talk and talk, but one mustn't take them seriously. Lower is lower, after all. . . . We are rabidly clerical and hierarchical. We deceive ourselves so easily about our benevolent concessions. What more do "they" want, after all? We, the bishops and, to some extent, the priests, know all about what needs to be done. . . . It is hard to get down to really living the idea that the charism of service demands a real commitment to listening and dialogue and walking elbow-to-elbow with others. (I would like to be able to share this sentiment with many others. I think that this is one spot where the church has failed the gospel, and one which calls for a profound conversion on our part, starting with Rome and filtering down to the humblest mission prelate and the most embryonic council of priests.)

Speaking of laypersons, I should once more recognize my debt to the cursillo movement. To the cursillos I also owe my encounter with the layman in the concrete, as a fellow traveler, as my equal in faith, as my equal in the common mission of the church, and as my equal in misery and in hope. All those unforgettable laypersons, men and women, from Catalonia, Spain, Guinea, and, occasionally, from America, who did so much to humanize my monkish, clerical, dehumanized humanity. People with whom I shared, more intimately than in many religious communities, "the wonders of grace," and with whom—through long days and nights—I "suffered" the church and tasted God, unforgettably.

Nowadays, when my friends in Brazil hear about my cursillista background, they either freeze or start poking fun at me. How is it possible that I—a free, reforming bishop, a leftist Christian in politics—could have been a cursillista, a cursillo "Padre," and even one of those who introduced the cursillos into Africa! When here, in Brazil and in America in general, the cursillos are looked upon as reactionary and angelistic. . . .

Of course, a great deal of water has flowed over the dam since the good old days of the cursillos of Mallorca and Creixell, and there is a long history to tell about the evolution and nonevolution of the "official" cursillos, and of their more or less classist introduction into Latin America, especially Venezuela.

The cursillos existed before the Council. Since the Council, the cursillos, especially in some aspects of the theology of grace and the "ecclesiology" of the world, have not kept in step with the new church. Changing styles, too much haste, and a too numerous membership have done the rest.

In the prelature of São Félix we don't have a single association or movement. Not because I reject them out of hand. I believe that our pastoral situation demands that we concentrate on forming that association of Jesus Christ which is his church. (When you get right down to it, I also learned to do just this in the good cursillos of better days.) I have worked in many associations and movements, and I have given myself over to their work with unstinting passion. Now I'm well enough on my way back.

Summing it all up, I cite a remark I wrote in my diary on October 18, 1970:

The national committee of the Legion of Mary in France has resigned. . . . All of these movements have their hour. I am thinking of the cursillos, too. They are worthwhile to the extent that they build church, according to the gospel and the signs of the times. The church survives them and surpasses them. The church creates them and gives them a history, an orientation towards an eternal future that is infinitely beyond all of them. No movement, congregation, council, century or "age" is the church. She is all of these and much more, both before and after.

4

I believe in the *religious life,* as an essential mark of the "evangelical" church. I have suffered a great deal in the cause of the religious life, and I have seen others do so. Yet I owe the religious life my present life in the church. I believe in the contemplative religious life, as well; I have always believed in it and I have even felt called to it at certain key moments in my life. And I gladly welcome all those new experiments in the religious life, including contemplative experiments, which are breaking out throughout the whole church of God, progressive and conservative, antiquated and prophetic, impossible and faithful.

But I think that the religious life has grown badly stiff-jointed and, in many sectors, has lost the train of its charism. I believe that institutes and orders should be far more thoroughgoing in self-renewal, more evangelically radical. I know that it is always easier to advise and request than it is to live and give. But I am stating what I believe in and what I would like to see become flesh in the church of Jesus.

I am going to copy here some passages from the "Suggestions" I sent, in January, 1973, to the meeting of Latin American Claretians which was being held at that time in Mexico:

We believe in "evangelical communities" (religious communities) which can and should be a sign and a ferment in the midst of the most diverse human environments: marginal people, unbelievers, frivolous and materialistic people; or in well organized churches that are in danger of becoming bureaucratic or apathetic or "worldly."

Nevertheless, we should demand that these communities be scandalously "evangelical," in the living of the beatitudes and in the proclamation of the goods that are to come.

All in all, we think that, given the church's present conditions and perspectives, as well as our own apostolic-missionary vocation, the (Claretian) congregation attempt and favor the establishment of "ecclesial communities" (understood as mixed communities made up of priests, religious and laity, both men and women).

We recommend these communities particularly in "mission countries" or in centers and environments designated as "mission" situations.

In any case, even strictly "evangelical" communities should be open, ecclesial and "worldly," i.e., committed to the life of the church in each place, and to the life—the struggles, hopes, monotony, housing, food, dress—of real, concrete, neighboring people.

An apostolate dedicated to propagating "our things" would be infantile, at best. What is needed is the vision, rhythm, and concrete action of each particular and local church.

"Our thing" is the church—the mystery of the world's salvation—together with the special, but always secondary, characteristics of the charism of our congregation.

I say "secondary," because what is "primary" in the church is common to all religious and all Christians.

These communities—evangelical as well as ecclesial—should be small, consisting of no more than six members. Communities with too many members not only hamper truly interpersonal relationships in community, but are also prevented from giving a witness to poverty and a spirit of welcome. They have a fatal tendency to turn into a group, a team, a residence, a market....

For both types of community, we feel that the present structure of the 'province' (or similar structures) is an insuperable object, which should be done away with.

Based on the theological importance of the particular church and the actual, local church, and operating within the functional framework of the national conference of bishops, our communities could form groups built around similar environments and services, under the coordination of some responsible person chosen by the bases involved. There would have to be some periodic meetings, either of the various coordinators or of different "evangelical" communities and the various members that make up "ecclesial" communities.

The present general government would become a general coordination, with members chosen from among the representatives of the bases, or by the representatives themselves, so as to be more sensitive to the calls of the church and the world, and so as to stimulate and channel interchanges and mutual help.

Doing all this, as rightly understood, would not signal the arrival of utopia or the outbreak of anarchy, nor would "evangelical" obedience be done away with. Of course, it would mean closing several houses, being much more selective about vocations, and giving up several buildings, enterprises, bonds, privileges, and nostalgias.

This would also put an end to certain "enclaves" of intercontinental dependence, to various colonialisms, provincialisms and greater or lesser centralisms. The entire bureaucracy of our various forms of religious government, the temptation to regard ourselves as a "perfect society" within the congregation or the church, and the antiwitness of being an enterprise or company—all these would have to go.

The manifestations of poverty, in any milieu, are forms of sharing the life of common people in that milieu: housing, clothing, food, work, travel, insecurity, and conflicts. . . .

And there should also be a great spirit of welcome, of neighborliness, of universal friendship, and of sociopolitical commitment.

For the sake of the kingdom. Without any other guarantee.

We must overcome the temptation to justify the "means" of the apostolate. The true means of the apostolate are supernatural, when you get right down to vivsecting things. "Natural" means will be valid to the extent that they do not contradict the gospel witness and the freedom of the Spirit: the being and the mission of the church.

From another point of view, in today's secularized society, the church—and the congregation, which is nothing if it is not church—must learn to get along without satisfying the itch to be all and know all in this world. Its mission is to be a leaven and a light in all things, no more, no less.

We need to take radical and urgent measures with

regard to goods and lifestyles. Otherwise we will stifle the Spirit and scandalize the world.

"Politics" are inevitable, because every human task is political. As González Ruiz says so well, in facing any situation the church (or one of us, or the community) can say "yes," or say "no," or say nothing. In all three cases, it adopts a political attitude. Political neutrality does not exist.

Our missionary charism obliges us to adopt a revolutionary attitude, in the sense of an evangelization that is clear, committed, and committing, one that renews consciousnesses and structures, and is incarnated in the anguish and aspirations of particular men and peoples.

Denunciation, renunciation (of privileges and marriage), and sometimes leadership (at least in the Spirit, in outlook and in risk-taking) are mandatory for the Claretian missionary, particularly here in Latin America, if he wants to be church here and now, in harmony with the conscious church of Latin America and of the whole Third World.

Not in the wake of all those who have no hope, but in front of them. (Or rather, at their side. With all those who are committed to the cause of man.) More "daring" than anyone else, because we have the force of the Spirit of the Risen Jesus.

We will doubtless provoke some scandals, some desertions. . . . But we have provoked many more over the centuries by taking the opposite attitude or by attempting to take none. Besides, these new "scandals" may well be prophetic and saving. We must liberate the oppressors by shaking up their consciences and shaking them out of the false security in which they are ensconced.

The kind of "adaptation" that we are asking for the "missions" should also be required for all activities in Latin America, where the church has been and still is, in many respects, an "import," a form of colonialism.

The culture, rights, struggles and aspirations of the people or communities we bring our mission to, should be something sacred and vital to us, something that takes precedence over our own ethnocentricity or formation, and over every ecclesiastical "discipline" or custom. (This does not mean denying the faith, or condemning that fundamental and truly Catholic kind of "discipline" which goes beyond the merely "Latin" or occidental.) Here, too, we should manifest our thoroughgoing missionary spirit.

I believe in celibacy and virginity, freely chosen, as an evangelical offering. As a form of poverty in the Spirit. As a Christian force which is a sign of eschatological witness, on the one hand, and of ecclesial availability, on the other. Nevertheless, I believe that in the future there will be both celibate and married priests. For the good of celibacy and for the good of the ministerial priesthood. God will not cease calling people to the charism of chastity for the sake of the kingdom, nor will the men and women of today and tomorrow cease responding to that call, just as the men and women of yesterday did.

Evangelical chastity is not a "discipline." It is a charism arising from within the calling to be a Christian.

5

Since the church is the People of God, we can more readily understand that it has to be the *People of Men,* "a light among the nations," as well as a "sign and instrument of the unity of the whole human race" (LG,1), and that "the joys and hopes, the griefs and anxieties of the men of this age, especially those who are poor or in any way afflicted," are also those of the church, and furthermore, that "all that is genuinely human finds an echo in its heart; finally, that "this community realizes that it is truly and intimately linked with mankind and its history" (GS, 1).

The church is "essentially mission." But it exists in the world and for the world. Its mission is to save the world, just as the Word became man and took upon himself the nature, the sin and the history of men, and for us men, died and rose.

The parables of the Kingdom—the yeast in the dough, the candle in the darkness, the seed in the earth—have always seemed so clear, so normal, and so demanding, to me.

God has willed the salvation of all. His Son died for all. The church is not a "perfect society," but the "perfecting" of human society. The church can't be the sort of "ghetto" that Israel tried to be. Christ formed his people and all peoples into "one" people, the People of God.

The church is the humanity that God loves and has tried to win: mysteriously on his part, freely on hers. The history of salvation mysteriously coincides with the history of the world. Just as there is but one, only God, so there is but one, only human history. The creator of man and of the universe is himself the redeemer and glorifier of man and of the universe. This conviction has continued to grow in me, so that today it is the cloudless horizon of my faith. It is my hope.

I, who was once tormented with the obsession of "saving" everyone possible, as soon as possible, "on the run," if you will—my missionary training and my experience with the cursillo movement contributed to this obsessive zeal— now believe, trustingly, that God saves according to his own rhythm and in many ways. "In a fragmentary manner," perhaps, "but in many ways," God keeps on talking to the world, "egged-on" by the saving presence of his Son, who died and rose for the world.

I still believe that the church is mission, and that the Lord's command to "go and proclaim" is still valid and urgent. I still believe in the seven sacraments, for example, as an historical expression of the sacramental being of the church itself. But I also believe in many other "contraband" sacraments which God can make use of, because I believe in Jesus Christ his Son, the savior of all mankind, the primordial sacrament, whose blood cannot have been slowed down to a small trickle for some favored few. I believe that the salvation of God often "works from within." I believe that everything is grace. I believe that grace is "greater" than the church, because grace is the universally saving Love of God, in Christ.

Whereas I once held that outside the church there is no salvation, I now believe that outside salvation there is no church:

> Perhaps (I wrote in my diary for 3/2/72) the newer and truer formulation of the old ecclesial adage should be: "Outside salvation there is no church!" The church exists only in saving; church is built only in the measure to which the world is saved!

The church cannot be just the ready-made, airtight room where the privileged celebrate salvation and make merry. The church is the open sign of salvation: the "official" place, yes, where salvation is celebrated—consciously, in community—a certain place, yes, but a place that is a point of departure, arrival, and encounter; a place of constant going-out. . . .

6

I have gotten to know the "other" churches, too.

The cause of ecumenism has become another of my suffering causes. For many years now I have been deeply wounded to witness how the prayer and testament of Jesus—"that all may be one"—has been so systematically ignored and blessedly taken for granted by Christians. The division that exists among Christians has always seemed to me to be the most absurd human division recorded in history. It is a sort of reverse mystery of faith, a sort of collective insanity of faith. It should not be, it must not be.

True, I was once a heated apologist, even a bizarrely Catholic one. The "divorcé" Henry VIII and the "hyena" Elizabeth I of England and the "apostate monk" Martin Luther, were all names and figures that I simply couldn't swallow.

Since then I have done a lot of reading and meditating. I have done a great deal of praying for unity and have asked many others to do so. And now I feel that ecumenism is something of a family cause.

I believe that I have overcome nearly all of my barriers. I say "nearly all." Who can say that he has overcome all of them? I am still exasperated by the fanaticism and proselytizing of certain nearby Protestants, just as I am by the fanaticism and proselytizing of certain Catholics: especially when either of them would shrink the Bible into some fossilized word, when they would make salvation the privilege of a select number of disembodied saints, and the church a sort of caste or ghetto. In my pastoral letter, *An Amazonian Church*, I spoke of the difficulties of "*sertão* ecumenism." It is easy to "do" ecumenism with real Christians. It's impossible with fanatics. And yet I think that even these fanatics deserve at least our fraternal understanding, because there are many factors that enter into anyone's "Christian" formation, and there are many forms of cultural and socio-economic conditioning that account for various kinds of fanaticism. On the other hand, we have nearly all been fanatical at one time or another.

I have very fond memories of my encounters with Taizé, that "city seated on a mountain": in an interview, I made for the *Iris de Paz;* in the person of Brother Bernardo from Olinda-Recife; from my readings of Roger Schutz and Max Thurian. I remember other readings, meditations, and lives of shining, committed Protestants. Then there was the passionate solidarity shown me by various Protestants in connection with the conflicts in my prelature; the retreat which Robert, a Lutheran seminarian, made with me in Crateús. In dialogue with many non-Catholic but real Christians, I have often found it easier to commune and express my feelings of communion, than in dialogue with many "Catholic" Christians, including priests and bishops. . . . What unites us more in Christ and in the mission of his church: the sharing of "manualized" Christian dogmas, or living our Christian faith together?

I know that the cause of unity, besides being a mystery of faith, is also a mystery of the cross, which we must all redeemingly bear until it is transformed into a paschal witness. And I know that the work of a few days is not going to undo the pride of centuries. But I do think that we might accelerate this cause, and I think that we should force its hour. Perhaps we're beating around the bush with orderly shared services, theatrical gestures and chats on doctrine and tradition, and are allowing ourselves the luxury of leaving up to the Holy Spirit alone, what we ourselves, depending on him, of course, should be doing ecumenically, with a little more freedom of faith and enough good will to make some historical reparations. Ecumenism isn't going to get done (nor has it) by just teaching justice or denouncing injustice, any more than the church can be built up by just proclaiming.

I hope that the churches are not going to spend their lives "imitating" the embraces of John XXIII and Athenagoras, or sending mutual observers to each other's meetings.

7

To the extent that the church is known as the sacrament of salvation and as the People of God, it is also recognized as being "particular" as well as "universal." Vatican II helped me, along with many others, to discover the *Good News of the Particular Church,* however imprecisely. Only later have I come to understand that the "signs of the times" should be complemented by the "signs of the places." Just as the new understanding of the nature and mission of the bishop transformed the ecclesiology of Vatican II, so my own episcopal ordination, and my consciousness and experience as a bishop, has profoundly modified the ecclesiology which I once professed and lived by. My recent theological and pastoral readings; the widespread attempts at founding *comunidades de base;* the overcoming of the heaven/earth dichotomy between a church that walks in the clouds and a humanity that steps into mud-puddles; a new, critical outlook that decentralized my view of the Church-Vatican monolith; my own "incarnation" among the People of God in whom I believe, with whom I suffer and to whom I commit myself right here, in the northwest of Mato Grosso, between the Araguaia and Xingu Rivers: All of these have been bringing me around to a new stance, to a new commitment vis à vis the real, daily mystery of the Particular Church.

In my pastoral letter, *An Amazonian Church,* I wrote:

> The church is by nature both catholic and local. "In order to be able to offer all of them the mystery of salvation and the life brought from God, the church must implant itself among all these groups for the same motive which led Christ to bind himself, in virtue of his incarnation, to the particular social and cultural circumstances of the men among whom he lived" (*Ad Gentes,* 10). Christ continues incarnating himself, through and with the church, in the concrete world of men in every time and place. God loves in the singular and he loves effectively. Salvation is made present in the day-to-day life and grasp of real men, principally by means of the church—"the universal sacrament of salvation"—to the extent that it approaches men in its testimony, in its "translation" of the Word into "now" language and in its sacraments adapted to real life; to the extent that it invites modern man to sincere conversion; and to the extent that it arouses in him—through the power of the Spirit, who is always ready to act—the response of a faith that transforms and liberates.
>
> We—your bishop, priests, Sisters, and lay team—are here, between the Araguaia and the Xingu, in this real

and concrete world, in this accusing, fringe world which I have just summarily described. And we are the "visible" and recognized church here. Either we make possible the saving incarnation of Christ in this milieu, or we deny our faith, are ashamed of the gospel, and betray the rights and the agonizing hopes of a human people who are also the People of God: the *sertanejos,* the *posseiros,* the *peones,* the Indians—this whole bit of Amazonian Brazil.

Because we are here, we must make our commitment here. Clearly. To the end.

This recognition of the church as "particular" and "local" involves some practical demands: in pastoral practice, in liturgy, in canon law (why not?) and in life. It involves its risks, too, and its drawbacks, both theoretical and practical.

I have already pointed out some of the alterations I would make, as regards the supreme pontiff, the Vatican, over-centralization, colonialism, and other power-positions in the church. It goes without saying that I believe in the pope as the visible rock of apostolic collegiality and ecclesial community, the ministerial cornerstone of communion in faith, as the one who should preside humbly and lovingly over the whole Christian people and their shepherds. Nevertheless, I do not believe in the Vatican as a state, as a "world-power," as a bureaucracy. It troubles me. It acts as a drag on the footsteps of the church of Jesus. I wish it would stop. I lament and reject all the titles, privileges, and benefices of bishops and priests and religious. One can "explain" all this as the baggage of history; but one cannot justify it. I believe that the gospel follows another route.

I say all this with an equal dose of respect and liberty.

If I am not contemplating an *ad limina* visit, it's because it would cost too much for travel and regalia, and because I would have to run too much interference in waiting rooms that I don't regard as "ecclesial." What I would like to be able to do, would be to meet simply and straightforwardly for a brother-to-brother talk with Paul, the bishop of Rome, who is, as I said, the ministerial cornerstone of the communion of all his people and their shepherds.

If I am at odds with the whole economic setup of the curia and with the way that setup is run—apart from the good will and expertise of its corps, of which I have no doubt—it is because here, in my own home-territory of this prelature, I have lived through and am still living through the contradictions and scandals which these entanglements produce, both among the people and among their ex-ploiters.

If I censure certain interventions of the nunciature, for example, which I have had to suffer more than once (as have some of my brother bishops), it is because I do not accept these interventions as a form of "church ministry," because I think that they are, at the very least, uncalled-for anachronisms; and because I discern in them the inter-ferences of diplomacy to the detriment of the gospel.

If I occasionally disagree with the Vatican or the presid-ing board of the National Council of Bishops, I do so despite my rank as a rural bishop, and I believe that any Christian, bishop or not, should be able to disagree. Be-cause I believe in the church as fraternal, as well as apos-tolic and hierarchical; as both a pilgrim in a state of search and conversion, and as divinely guaranteed in the Spirit; as particular, and at the same time, universal.

I also find it to be a perfectly Christian thing, for example, for a priest of the diocese of Rome to feel free to write the pope a letter about the Holy Year; or that some conscientious Catholics from the Balearic Islands in the Mediterranean should feel free to do likewise; or that the priests and laity of the church of Viana in Maranhão should represent their feelings and wishes previous to the appointment of their new bishop.

St. Cyprian told his priests: "I do not wish to do anything merely on the basis of my own opinion, without taking into account your consent and that of the people."

We have all heard, and with good reason, the oft-repeated adage, "Nothing without the bishop." Now we should hear, just as frequently, the adage, "Nothing without the people."

I'm not asking for pipe-dreams. The pope or any bishop can have his curia, let us say. But what I would ask for is that such a group should change its style: less "curial" and more "evangelical." I am also well aware that centuries of historic precedent can not be done away with overnight. But I believe in the Spirit's power to make even these "things new," without having to wait until the parousia.

Where there is a greater clarity, simplicity and corresponsibility in faith, there will also be a correspondingly greater freedom of spirit, word, and action.

Those "on top" (I even include myself, somewhat, in that group) will have to get used to listening to what their brothers "on the bottom" have to say. And those who are "on the bottom" will have to more free, frequent, responsible, and risk-taking, in exercising their right to speak up to those above them and alongside them. And those below will have to concede to those above, their own freedom and responsibility, and their special ministry of feeding God's flock (which is a human flock of human beings, who are sons of God, and not just a pack of sheep!).

And both of us will have to get used to walking together, side by side, on the same level of fraternal communion, without so many aboves and belows, accepting in practice the fundamental equality of all the baptized, favoring in fact the exercise of pluralism within the unity of the faith, and pleasing God and man by giving rein to the free and enriching interplay of a dialogue between the church and the world.

This fraternal attitude of listening and dialogue and freedom will in no way prejudice the hierarchical structure of the church, although it will restrict it to its proper confines, as a safeguard and stimulus of harmony in faith and charity within the body, and of apostolic service to the community of believers and the world of men.

I repeat once more my declaration that I say all this with such vehemence, because this church that I dearly love, also pains me deeply.

8

During this profession of my faith, I have occasionally mentioned the saints. I have never felt that I should do without them. I believe that they have never interfered to the detriment of my relations with Christ or with God. I believe that the saints and, in particular, the holiest of them all—Mary, the mother of Jesus—have positively helped me to discover and love the living and true God and Jesus Christ, his Son.

To be sure, I've come a long way in my view of the saints and Mary, and in my dealings with them. And I owe much of this to Vatican II.

I believe that the fundamental advance in my devotion to Mary and to my already glorious brothers and sisters came with the realization that in the consciousness of faith and the communion of hope, the church of the here and the church of the beyond are identified as one, single church of living continuity and vital intercommunion; it came with seeing the "Jerusalem on high" as the Jerusalem here below, too; it came with believing in the triumphant church as simply the pilgrim church coming into its fullness, glorified with Christ in God, forever.

Even in my childhood the thought of the saints moved me: their lives, their witness, their feastdays. I have always enjoyed praying the "Communicantes" in the first eucharistic prayer.

I have my preferences, my "particular friendships" among them, for reasons of temperament, formation—or simply, by the free law of friendship: Abraham, the patriarch of all who are called, the emigrant of faith; Isaiah, the lyricist of messianic times, the evangelist-prophet—and the other prophets and leaders committed to Yahweh and the people; John the Baptizer, the precursor who could not be bought off, selfless to the point of death; Joseph, the companion of Mary and the "*pai de criaçao*" (stepdad) of Jesus, the hero of silence and day-by-day fidelity; the apostles of Jesus, Peter, above all, and John and Paul; Stephen, the first martyr; Lawrence, the jovial witness from Huesca; Ignatius of Antioch, bishop and martyr; Augustine, all heart and fiery word—and other Fathers and shepherds of the church; Francis of Assisi, poet, mystic, beggar who overcame the strongholds of power and money; Francis Xavier, the missionary; the founder of my own congregation, Anthony Mary Claret, a burning, realistic apostle; Teresa of Avila and Therese of Lisieux, friends and teachers; Maximilian Kolbe, the madman of our Lady and victim of a concentration camp; then, Brother Charles de Foucauld, incessant searcher for God in the desert of prayer and among the men of the desert; and so many others, canonized or to be canonized. . . .

Among my friends I have a repuation for being "Marian."

And really, I have counted heavily on the Blessed Virgin in my life. I have spoken and written a great deal about her. I have prayed to her frequently, and meditated on her. I have felt her quite present. I love her. I confide in her.

I believe in Mary, the Poor Woman of Yahweh, the immaculate one, full of grace, ever virgin, mother of the Son of God, Jesus Christ, maternally associated in the life and death of her Son, singularly glorified in her assumption, type and mother of the church.

From the hermitage of the fortress overlooking my home town—with its slopes of *"romaní i farigola"* (rosemary and thyme)—through all the Marian hermitages and shrines of my seminary formation and my ministry, I have brought my pilgrim fervors and even my tears. To cite but a few, I would have to include la Mare de Déu del Castellvell at Solsona, la Mare de Déu de la Salut at Sabadell, la Virgen del Pueyo at Barbastro.

Then there are the patronal titles I have given to various churches in the prelature: la Asunción, Our Lady of the *Posseiros*, Our Lady of the Vision, Our Lady of Liberation. . . .

Both as a seminarian and a priest I did some of the craziest things for Mary, such as visiting her shrines; spending nights and rest-periods writing radio programs, articles, poems, and book on Mary; sponsoring pilgrimages to Fatima, or on the occasion of the defining of the Assumption, or the Marian Year; or promoting Marian devotion on significant occasions, such as congresses, commemorations, consecrations, etc., of this "Age of Mary," in which I have, happily, lived. I have written *Nuestra Señora del siglo XX* (Our Lady of the Twentieth Century). I have written some biblical-social poems, *Llena de Dios y de los Hombres* (Full of God and Men). I have written a number of programs and articles for radio and for various reviews. I collected, in "litanies of former times" and in "litanies of the last moment," all the possible Marian titles I could find, until I ended up with a song to "Holy Mary without any more titles":

> After talking so much about you,
> I almost hush now,
> in tune with the voice of your own silence.
> (Saying your "fiat" and yielding your womb.
> Singing, gratefully, on the mountaintop,
> for all the wide winds of history to hear
> the joyful song of the poor made free.
> And then withdrawing, silent, behind the gospel ...
> Giving the world its Man-Redeemer
> Giving the Son back to the Father.) Hail, Mary,
> —March 25th and Mato Grosso—
> Mother of the Word, in silence!

I had a passion for Mariology. I studied the thick volumes of *"Estudios Marianos,"* by The Spanish Mariological Society, and other Mariological treatises. And I believe that I got a good, solid, lasting foundation in Marian teaching, along its main lines: Mary and Christ, Mary and the bible, Mary and grace, Mary and the church.

I should mention one little "golden book" which was a milestone along my Marian way: *Mary and the Church,* by Hugo Rahner.

As the years have gone by—with the coming of the new theology in the new church, after Vatican II; with my Christian experience of social struggle; with the poverty of environment and spirit that have eaten into me here in this Mato Grosso—my faith in Mary has become more naked, more free, and more true. And more and more she has become, in my mind and in my heart, the songstress of the Magnificat, the prophetess of the poor made free, the mother of the people, the outcast mother in Bethlehem, in Egypt, in Nazareth, and among the great ones of Jerusalem. Mary is "she who has believed," and is hence blessed; "turning over in her heart," in the silence of faith (without vision, without much advance knowledge), the things, the deeds, the sayings of her Sons. The mother of the one who was persecuted by all of the powerful. The sorrowful mother of the crucified. The most conscious witness of the Passover. The most authentic Christian of Pentecost. A great, eschatological sign in the midst of the People of Hope. . . .

Here in Mato Grosso, within the framework of this new attitude toward Mary, I wrote this *Prayer to Our Lady of the Third World:*

Pilgrim sister of the Poor of Yahweh,
Prophetess of the poor made free,
Mother of the Third World,
mother of all men in this world that is one
because you are the Mother of God made man.

With all those who believe in Christ
and with all those who in any way seek his Kingdom,
we call on you, Mother,
to talk to him for all of us.

Pray to him—him, who became poor
to share with us the riches of his Love—
so that his church may strip herself,
without subterfuge,
from all other riches.

Ask him, who died upon the cross to save mankind,
that we, his followers,
might learn to live and die
to wholly free our brothers.

Ask him that we be devoured
by the thirst and hunger for that justice
which strips and saves us.

Ask him who felled the wall of separation
that all of us who bear the seal of his name
may seek in deed,
beyond all barriers that divide,
that unity which he himself laid claim to as his testament,
and which is only possible within the freedom of the sons
    of God.

Ask him who, risen, lives beside the Father,
to send us the joyous power of his Spirit,
that we may learn to overcome our selfishness, routine, and
    fear.

Country mother, working mother,
born in a colony
and martyred by legalism and hypocrisy:
teach us to read, sincerely, the gospel of Jesus
and translate it into life

with all its revolutionary consequences,
with all the radical spirit of the Beatitudes
and in the total risk of Love that knows how to give ones
    life for those one loves.

Through Jesus Christ,
your Son,
The Son of God, our Brother.

I am speaking of the church. It hasn't escaped my attention. But as my poet-friend, St. Ephraem, wrote: "The earth of the church is the body of Mary."

IV

The Cause
of the New Man

1

At home I was suckled on austerity. "Nosaltres som pobres, fills—Children, we are poor," we were often told by my father and mother. I was also taught, at home, to have a certain contempt for the rich, for ill-gained goods, for ill-spent money, and for showiness. Even as a child, luxury was always offensive to me, and I have always been outraged by exploitation. I saw within my own family how greed can divide. I later came to see how opportunistic and disloyal politics can be.

As I have already said, we were right-wingers. None of us could have been anything else. The right wing stood for religion, good, order and virtue.

I used to hear Primo de Rivera's dictatorship described with such glowing nostalgia, that it made me think that dictatorship was a desirable thing.

Socialism, communism, and all the "isms" of the left were all jumbled together in my right-wing young eyes as a thing of horror. As I looked at them—through scenes of profanations and deaths, of fire and blood, of closed shutters and threatening rifle shots, of the whispers of grown-ups and the hidden life of the "draft-dodgers," and unfrocked priests and nuns—all these "isms" could only appear to me as the most monstrous sort of anarchy.

Naturally, I knew nothing evil about the other side of the coin. (Perhaps the worst thing I knew, unconsciously, was that there *were* two sides.) The Nationalists would bring us liberation, the return of peace, the chance to practice our religion in public again. "When the Nationalists come... !" In any case, whenever something had to be justified in those days, there was always one saying to fall back on: "That's war!"

I was somewhat shocked at seeing the arrival of refugees fleeing from the Nationalists. But then if they were Reds, it was only natural for them to flee.

Nevertheless, I used to sing some communist songs. They were in the air. And they left a certain taste of forbidden fruit in my mouth: "¡Arriba, parías de la Tierra! /¡En pie los obreros sin pan! / ¡Arriba los Pobres del Mundo! /¡Viva la Internacional!. / . Hijo del Pueblo, que oprimen cadenas: / Esta injusticia no puede seguir; / si tu existencia es un mundo de penas / antes que esclavo, prefiere morir!... Los hombres han de ser hermanos..." (Up, you outcasts of the earth! On your feet, breadless workers! Up, you poor of the world! Long live the International!... Son of the people, oppressed by chains, this injustice cannot go on; if your existence is a world of pain, then choose death to slavery!... Men must all be brothers...). "Hearty" words that stood for a cause and spoke of the great, wide world.

I also learned the Nationalist songs and in my own poetically precocious way, savored their blue, Spanish verses. Nevertheless, I do recall some grave reservations by my father and "l'oncle Josepet" (it was right in front of the cemetery), about two verses from the *Himno de los Regulares:* "Cada uno será lo que quiera, / nada importa su vida anterior. . . . Each man will be what he wishes to be,/ no matter what his previous life. . . ."

Then came the Nationalists and my whole perspective started breaking up again. The Reds were bad, but the Nationalists were by no means totally good. On top of it all, the Nationalists were the army, and "Castilians"; and they brought a great deal of immorality and irresponsibility along with them. The "Moors" robbed people and pulled the fillings out of dead men's teeth; and the officers made their decrees with a repellent sort of superiority.

As the war had had its wild imaginings, so the postwar had its disillusionments. It came by degrees. They bought me a Falangist uniform—blue shirt, black leather belt, red beret—because it was the fashion to be Falangist at that time. But I never wore it. So many people went Falangist and won important posts just by changing their shirt. So many irresponsible people. I got myself a traditionalist medal in protest. The traditionalists were more "on God's side"; they had to be the most chemically pure Nationalists—the ones who kept the sacred national image alive. . . .

In the seminary—especially the minor seminary—the Reds were always represented to us as an absolute evil. The Claretian congregation had more victims than any other religious group in the persecution of 1936; some of them, such as the community at Barbastro, bore all the marks of true martyrdom.

The "allies" of the Nationalists were watched with great sympathy during World War II: Hitler's Germans were the opponents of Russian communism. The deeds of the Blue Division colored our history classes with snow white and blood red. We knew nothing of the dreadful side of

Nazism. The "Caudillo" (Franco) was, in any case, one sent from God.

We became conscious of our own self-deceptions by way of the tales of "our war" that came from within, from conversations among friends, from our first contacts with street life with its labor problems and centralist controls, from the discrimination that was practiced between some Spaniards and others, and from the attitudes and timid— very timid—statements from certain sectors of the church that began to disagree with the unconditional blessing of Cardinal Gomá and started demanding the rights of freedom of the press, freedom of assembly, and justice for the worker.

It was a very slow and highly conditioned awakening.

I began to meet a socialist or communist (an "ex" of course) here and there, not as a soldier, but as a man of flesh and bone and spirit. In the cursillos I made friends with a number of them. From this coign of vantage, I could see all the fanaticism and crimes of Fascism and Nazism. I might add, in passing, that I now became aware of, and was deeply moved by "the Jewish question." This was an historic blot that I could not forgive—and still cannot forgive—the church and the world.

The regime was becoming more and more of a burden to me. It was lasting longer than we had bargained for. Spain was getting to be altogether too "different." Europe and the rest of the world were there, and they were well worth the trouble. National Socialism and National Catholicism and all the national and vertical "isms" were getting to be too much for me, because they were publicly omnipresent and adulterated even the purest values. And, let me tell you, a critical consciousness, in a religious house in Spain, especially outside Catalonia, was something that was bought at the price of swallowing buckets of saliva, in those days.

I was now witnessing the hovels of Sabadell, Barcelona, and Madrid, and the tragedy of internal and external migration, and the problems of labor, and the asphyxiating lack of liberty, even as regarded the publication of some timid little article in a provincial review. When I was director of the *Iris de Paz*, the police were involved even in the publication of a simple account. Freedom was a climate for which there was no substitute. Order couldn't be bought at any price. Not all the public works in the world could justify keeping a whole nation in a state of perpetual minority.

2

The awakening of Africa won me over to its cause, and unmasked for me the camouflaged colonialisms that I once thought of as discovery and evangelization. America was no longer just one more glory of Spain's great navigators. True, I knew a sad side of Fidel Castro's Cuba through some young exiles who came to Madrid and whom I befriended. But I also knew enough about Batista's Cuba, Yankee imperialism's Cuba, the Cuba of Latin American cutthroats. And I knew about the hunger, the illiteracy, and the exploitation of the New World and of the whole Third World and its people, by the first and second worlds.

In Guinea I learned many things at first hand. And I remember the bitter confidences of certain black leaders and the blame they laid on the whites, the missionaries.

Since then I have fully grasped and felt the whole rotten myth of racist superiority, divinely-decreed eminent domain and inhuman exploitation that has gone into the discovery, colonization, and, at times, even the evangelization of the New World. "Colonization" and "civilization" are words that I no longer regard as part of a human vocabulary. Nor, where I live and suffer, are the new colonialist slogans of "pacification" and "integration" of the Indians. In my credo, imperialism, colonialism, and capitalism deserve an anathema. I loath the monuments in honor of the discoverers and *bandeirantes.* I become physically ill when I see the monument to Anhanguera in the public square of Goiânia. It would upset me even more to see a monument to Las Casas or to "the unknown *sertanejo.*" And I would love to see a much more critical purge of the histories of the colonized people and the history of the Christian missions. When I read *Bury my Heart at Wounded Knee,* I was once more—pardonably—ashamed of being "occidental," "Spanish," and "Christian," because it reminded me of so many deeds perpetrated by the penetration of civilization. . . .

It is because one lives so close to certain things. It is because one has historical consciousness, without the wherewithal to react.

I am well aware that the roots of colonialism are sunk deep and stubborn in us, like a second nature of ethnocentric superiority. We are the "good guys"; while these "poor people" to whom we have been sent. . . . And we have not—not by a long shot—seen the end of ecclesiastical colonialism (if I may be excused for displaying some of our own dirty laundry). In theology, in liturgy, in law, in pastoral theology, we are thoroughgoing Europeans, intellectualists, Latins, Romans and, to top it off, adherents of this or that religious order, or this or that church of origin.

I am getting carried away again. I would like to say something, so many things, about the Indians and of the desperate outcry their cause deserves. Something, too, of the impassioned faith with which I am committed to this "lost cause." Toward the beginning of 1974, after braving the censorship here and working miracles to find paper and a press, twelve of us bishops and missionaries from different indigenous regions in Brazil got together and published "an urgent manifesto on the dramatic plight of the indigenous peoples of Brazil," which bore the significant title, *Y-JUCA-PIRAMA* (The Indian: He Who Must Die). I have to refer to this paper, because it is a manifesto of my faith in the Indian cause. I begin with a quote from page 24, where an old Tapirapé from our vicariate asks a missionary:

"How much have the (agro-cattle) companies paid your Heavenly Father, to make him give them the lands of the Indians?"

And the following commentary:

The Christian will be a universal sign of salvation and a revealer of the love of the Heavenly Father in all places, but especially among indigenous people, only if he is a respectful, patient, and hope-giving presence, capable of perceiving, living, and revealing the genuine values of these people, in which the millennial action of God in their lives has been expressed. This would be a proper observance of the continuity of Christ's incarnation.

Read the document stating the conclusions of the American Indian Parliament of Cono Sur, held at San Bernardino, Paraguay, from the 8th to the 14th of October, 1974. And read the statements of more recent meetings of native *caciques* or tribal leaders in Brazil, in the rest of Latin America and in North America. Be aware of the new awareness, the new sense of self-identity that these nations now feel. It will not be easy to stifle the will for respect and the imperatives for self-affirmation that are being awakened among the most far-flung sectors of the Amerind people. Pastoral theology and practice toward these populations, thank God, is also awakening, and there are many of us missionaries who sincerely and humbly wish to put an end to "colonizing" in the name of the gospel. . . .

3

As a child I hated to see anyone firing even a peashooter at sparrows. I have never fired a gun and hope I never shall. War—since I lived through it as a child—is never likely to win any enthusiasm from me. *Jeux interdits* (Forbidden Games) is one of the movies that have made the deepest impression on me. Oh, I was sometimes moved—through the glorifying lens of history—by the "great" wartime feats of the past, and I felt some sympathy for their heroes. I had (and even still have, at a distance) good friends in the military.

At a distance, I say. Here, closer to home, the soldiers

are my "enemies," especially to the extent that they are enemies of the people. Because they are at the service of capitalism and the dictatorship; because they are servilely committed to cover-up welfare schemes, impact studies, repression, and even torture. I'm not talking second-hand; I'm talking about what I've seen.

Although I haven't yet come up with a finished formula for what to say—in the real, anguishing heat of practice—about violence, I know that I hate weapons more than ever, and I would like, some day, to see all armies retired and their "swords beat into ploughshares and their spears into pruning hooks."

I can't imagine how everyone seems to be able to tolerate the suicidal, collective madness of the arms-race or the staggering military budgets or repression. It seems like one more proof of a universal lack of human feeling when we can stand by—in the most "natural" diplomatic and providentialist indifference—at the macabre spectacle of Vietnam or Biafra, or the starving millions in Asia, or the genocide of so many peoples and races. If I want to believe in humanity, if I want to believe in the faith, I can't see how we can "diplomatically" or "providentially" put up with governments and trusts doing what they please with the goods and lives of the people, or that the church is interested in "antiseptic" dialogues with so many exploiting powers. Is it for the good of the "institutional church," or is it for the service of a redeemed mankind? I simply ask.

A few weeks ago I was visited and interrogated by federal agents of the government from Brasilia. In response to my accusations about the social problems of the region, one of them remarked that I was speaking "com muito colorido—much too colorfully." That may well be so. Maybe I am a romantic and a demagogue. Maybe I am thinking and talking like a dreamer. But if that's the case, I hope to God I never "come to my senses!"

I believe that nowadays the only way to live is to live rebelliously. And I believe that you can only be a Christian by being a revolutionary, since there's no more use in pretending that we're going to "reform" the world. All the disembodied providentialisms, neoliberalisms, neocapitalisms, neodemocracies or other careful reform movements which either deceive or are deceived—cynically or stupidly—serve only to protect the privileges of the privileged few, at the price of the submissive productivity of the many who are dying of hunger. And, by this very fact, they seem to be involved in objective iniquity.

One thing I have come to learn clearly from life: right-wingers are reactionary by nature, fanatically unbending when it comes to saving their own slice of the pie, and utterly united in defending the "law and order" that keeps them a perpetual minority.

What more is there to say?

No *Politics* is definitively written. The politics of a country or of the world, like the life of a person, is worked out step by step, day by day. I do know that I have somehow passed from the anarchist horror of my childhood to adopt some sort of socialist options. By my contacts with the dialectic of life, by the demands of the gospel, and by some of the good points of Marxism. What kind of socialism, I'm not quite sure; any more than I'm sure of what kind of church will result tomorrow from our efforts at building one today—although I do know that we want it to be more and more Christian; any more than I know what that Utopia (which, in my hope, I believe to be a reality) toward which mankind, stirred by the Spirit of the Risen Jesus, is heading, is really like.

"But," people frequently ask me, "can't you see that so-cialism, too, has never really succeeded anywhere?"

And I answer with the question: "But don't you see that socialism hasn't really been tried? Don't you see that the gospel has not yet been lived socially? And that the New Commandment has not yet had its debut, politically?"—I add.

The socialism which I, and many other brothers in the faith and in the passion for justice, are fighting for—as being the best socio-political instrument available to us today for the transformation of human society—is not precisely the socialism of this or that regime, let alone this or that party. It certainly isn't Russia or Cuba or China or Algeria or Allende's Chile. But it has some of their good points.

God knows I'm not fighting for any sort of dictatorship whatsoever. I believe, with Lord Acton, that "power tends to corrupt, and absolute power corrupts absolutely."

In my attempt at being a Christian, I know that I can and ought to go far beyond communism. Moreover, I have, for many years now, felt very little enthusiasm for the world of international communism. After reading Sol-zhenitsyn, for example, no one could have any great illu-sions about the Soviet paradise. Nevertheless, I am much less enthusiastic about the capitalist paradises where most people live in the Siberia of hunger or of the slavery or madness of the consumer society. It was the people's people—not the mandarins, the reverends, the great ladies, the families with social position, or the owners—who gained from what Castro, Allende, or Mao accom-plished. And if politics is the art of the common good, then I believe that the common good is more legitimate to the extent that it is more "common."

I hope that Panikkar will forgive me, but I think that

capitalism is "intrinsically evil," because it is nothing more than socially institutionalized egoism, the public worship of lucre for lucre's sake, the official recognition of the exploitation of man by man, and the slavery of the many under the yoke of the interest and prosperity of the few.

During the interrogation to which the pastoral team of the prelature was submitted, the presiding officer at the trial inquired insistently about my socialism and what I meant by socialization. (This latter word was ferreted out, as a "corpus delicti," from some of the writings that the police and the army had confiscated among our belongings.) To avoid getting into any long and involved arguments, since that was hardly the time or the place for them, I answered:

> For me, Dr. Francisco, socialization means the greatest possible sharing by all citizens, within the greatest possible equality, in all the goods "of nature and culture." (I borrowed the expression between quotes from Paulo Freire, whose teachings and methods on popular education also formed part of the "corpus delicti" of our inquest.)

He limited himself to remarking (as so many of his stamp do) that this sort of socialization was a mere Utopia. I answered:

> "I said 'possible,' Dr. Francisco. At any rate, my hope really is utopian, in the sense that it will never be perfectly realized here, in the earthly city...."

And yet, I would like to add here, that the whole Christian life should be a "realization" of this Utopia. We are en route to the heavenly city only to the extent that we strive "utopianly" to establish it here, in the brutish streets of the earthly city. Anyone who refuses to build the world of the new man here below, with the political materials available to us in the here and now, is ipso facto castrating his belief in the practice of social life (which is what politics is), and is refusing to build the kingdom of God, which is also a fraternal community, an effective equality and real sharing of goods. The new commandment is radically socializing. The gospel itself is the subversion of interests, because it is the demolition of idols. Who can fit social classes into the constitution of the kingdom? At our trial, Eugenio and I gave a copy of the New Testament to the presiding official and his recording secretary. It was inscribed as follows: "Um dia a Palavra de Deus fará o inquerito de todos nós." (Some day the Word of God will make inquiry of us all.) Earlier, Eugenio had told Dr. Francisco that the police had passed over the "most subversive" book we had in the house. . . .

Summing up, I believe that the socialization of the world can be a real attempt to live Christianly in society. And I believe that capitalist society is a radical denial of this attempt. Capitalism cannot be Christian; socialism can. If tomorrow there should emerge some better scheme allowing us to be Christians politically—to be Christians in real life, which is always political—then we Christians should adopt this better scheme. And thus, by possible and concrete steps, we walk on until we reach the Parousia. Amen.

4

I have already remarked that I have not figured out an adequate statement of my position on violence and nonviolence. I confess that I don't like speaking about either of them. I would much rather talk about justice, liberty, and love, as a program. When violence and nonviolence is discussed, the first and worst kind of violence—the institutionalized, officially justified, diplomatically tolerated and dialogued sort—blasts away, and then provokes a reaction of so many other, lesser forms of violence. This is the "spiral of violence" of which our dear Dom Hélder speaks.

Clearly, I would not even like to see a flower petal "violated." I am allergic to violence, both by temperament and by faith. I believe in the universal Love of God, the Father of all men. I believe in the new commandment of Jesus. I believe in forgiving one's enemies and, by that very fact, I believe in everyone loving everyone else, and in the brotherly love that is every single human's due. And I can also assure you that this belief in charity has cost me a heap of suffering.

I don't think I've ever "hated" anyone. I have never rejoiced in the death of anyone or wished anyone "ill." I have, indeed, more than once wished that certain enterprises, plans, governments, and powers would fail. I still do. And more than once I have felt the most consuming anger. As early as October 29, 1969, I wrote in my diary:

> I am building up a huge reserve of contempt and anger for this sort of exploiting, self-serving politics. . . . If I don't know how to do something about it or am unable to do something about it, if I can't find a way to speak about it or give some living testimony against it, then give me, Lord, at least the "minimum" grace of liberating someone through my death. . . .

Among my other passions, I have this passion of anger, I think it might even be a sort of exasperated "sacrament" of my love for my neighbor. Setting aside my own modest

anger, the anger of the prophets and the anger of Jesus
were, in their own day and way, a sacrament of the inward
fire of their zeal for the glory of God and the dignity of
man.

I know that a certain amount of anger can be the prod-
uct of one's liver, or the result of one's social powerlessness
to resolve the tragedies that are staring him in the face, or
a reaction in the face of the passivity and "independent"
coexistence of the powerful and institutions.

At any rate, I don't know how to say anything that will be
of much help to someone who feels the sting of oppression
in his own house or his hide:

> I've been thinking and rethinking, these days, about
> what sort of attitude towards social struggle could be
> truly Christian and, therefore, realistic and true. I don't
> say "efficient," in the sense of technical, lucrative, or
> immediate effectiveness. I know that it is a struggle that
> takes place in time and aims at an eschatological goal. I
> keep thinking that the terms "violence" and "nonvio-
> lence" miss the mark. Justice and love more fully define
> the true Christian attitude of a life committed to the
> renewal of the world.
>
> Speaking of "nonviolence" always seems like speaking
> of "nonwar" when you mean peace. "Nonviolence" is
> said with relationship to "violence." It would be better to
> talk of "justice" and "just means." But *which* means? And
> when are they to be used? And to what extent? This is
> the problem of conscience that faces every individual,
> every hour of the day. Which is not to say that there
> cannot be some basic church teaching or criteria on the
> matter.
>
> Perhaps we need to work out a better definition of

legitimate self-defense. I'd know quite well what to hold if I were speaking of my own, personal defense. Dying would be an easy solution, as applies to me personally. But it's not so clear that I could ask it of the father of a family or a people. Would we have to start talking about collective "martyrdoms"? I don't know. The theologians will have to do a great deal of thinking about the "theology of revolution" (and nonviolence). And all of us—"violent," "nonviolent" and "neither/nor"—will have to do a lot of dialoguing yet.

"If you want peace, work for justice." This, in any case, is a valid formula. (*Diary:* June 7, 1972)

I lament the existence of guerrilla warfare and admire the (utopian?) generosity of many guerrillas, but, above all, I inexorably condemn the causes that provoke guerrilla warfare. And, in principle, a guerrilla seems worthier to me than a dictator.

God knows how much I have prayed and sought for *peace:*

> The peace I always seek.
> The peace I never find.
> The strange peace of God that bears me
> like some creaking, joyful boat.
> The peace I give, making my blood trickle,
> like thick milk. . . .

And yet, all of this notwithstanding, I have also written, during these days of conflict (suffering, persecution, and repression), that the very word "peace" smacks to me of inertia, interested complicity, and angelism. And in fact, all too frequently, peace has been a synonym for the established order, when justice alone is the old and new name for peace. "Peace, peace, peace and there is no peace," says the Lord, because there is no justice. Can anyone be blessed for seeking peace if, at the same time, he does not seek justice with a burning thirst? I know that Christ speaks of that justice which is the glory of the living God, but it is also the glory of the living man! Just as he speaks of the first commandment, which is also the second! I know that "no one can speak of justice unless he himself is just," but can anyone speak of peace unless he wears himself out trying to build it in justice?

I believe, in any case, that "He is our Peace." And I appeal to him in the last instance, while in the first instance I dirty my hands and muddy my heart in the ooze and outcry of the daily struggle for Justice on the part of so many brothers. "Struggle and Contemplation" was the theme of the Youth Council held at Taizé, one August. Philippe, 22 years old, who lives among the gypsies of Grenoble, commented on it as follows: "Struggle is a means. The end is the encounter with God. But this encounter is impossible without justice."

5

Because of my reactionary training, liberty always sounded like a pamphlet slogan to me. During the revolution, we heard tell of various "libertarian" movements. In much the same way, "honor" and "duty" have often sounded to me like nineteenth-century passwords from the military code.

Since then, I have read some history and seen a bit. I have lived with the fleshly bondage of many brethren for whom I feel directly responsible. And I have lived to experience, in my own household, dictatorship, censorship, repression, jail, and torture.

Now I believe in liberty! And I believe in it as a supreme good of one who has been made in the image and likeness of God. I believe in the liberty of man which God himself mysteriously respects.

I believe in freedom of thought and religion. I believe in the freedom of the press and of the arts and of culture. I believe in freedom of assembly. I believe in the freedom of ethnic minorities.

I believe that man's freedom is more than socio-political. And I know quite well that no man can muzzle human freedom. No system, no repressive machine, can gauge its spiritual and sovereign depths.

But I also know that man is society and that he depends on society in order to realize himself as man. Those few who are truly free are liberated even more in a climate of enslavement; but it cows or brutalizes or disheartens the many who are hardly free in the drowned roots of their human condition.

If we are to live humanly, we need social and political freedom. Where there is no freedom there is no justice. Where there is no justice there is no human society.

If I remember correctly, the review *El Ciervo*—a good partner for dialogue in this part of the world—began a series in the form of dialectical game in which justice and freedom took opposite sides. I am on the side of both, naturally. But, should the inevitable conflict between them arise, I would be bold enough to add the following rule— which is theoretically sound and which we should make sure is put into practice—to the game (so as to avoid the occurrence of what one Brazilian comedy states: "Theory in practice is something else."):

The public exercise of individual liberty can only be curtailed in favor of the true demands of community justice.

"My freedom begins where the freedom of everyone else begins." And my freedom ends where the justice of others demands.

6

I believe that God has handed creation over to the intelligence and the hands of man. "Fill the earth and subdue it," said the Lord. I believe in work, in science, in technology, and in progress. I am neither a troglodyte, a medievalist, nor some sort of idyllic Rousseauvian. I recognize that humanity has come a long way, thank God and man for that! Some years ago, a group of illustrious Spaniards were asked to choose their "ideal" century. Some chose the thirteenth, the sixteenth, and even the eighteenth. I am with José María Pemán in choosing the twentieth century. Like Maragall's Barcelona, "With all its sins, it's at least ours."

Nevertheless, now that we are on the subject of freedom, I would have to dedicate a whole bitter elegy to the civilization, progress, science, technology, development, production, consumerism, urbanism, publicity, security, etc., of this, our beloved and rotten society, which needs to be reborn in the simplicity of the primitives, the freedom of the poor and the joy of the little ones. And in the grace of the gospel of Jesus Christ!

François de Closets has published a book, *Le bonheur en plus*, which ponders on a number of things we think on—when we think: Progress doesn't make us more human, and hence it doesn't make us any happier. The great lie of our civilization is the invention of the producer-consumer, who seeks his happiness in consumer goods. "I cannot understand," says de Closets, "how the Catholic church, for example, has let this pass without more of a protest since, as I see it, this is a radical perversion which betrays man himself."

To cite one more example, I would like to recommend that my readers page through Arturo Paoli's book on *The Roots of Man*. I would also like to recommend a respectful visit to the Tapirapé village and then, by way of contrast, a visit to São Paulo or a critical look-in at a society party or a circle of magnates or politicians. I recommend a real live-in with a working family or any other long enough experience of real poverty. But above all, I recommend a fully conscious dip into the raging waters of your own heart. . . . After that, you'll feel like urging God to re-create all things, to build a society of human beings upon the ruins of this society of electronic sleepwalkers, and a heart of flesh upon the powdered ashes of our heart of stone!

7

In the credo that gave meaning to his life, Javier Domínguez, whose faith in justice I fully share, writes:

> Fr. Díez Alegría fairly scandalized the ears of some people when he wrote: "Marx led me to rediscover Christ and the meaning of his message." Exactly the opposite happened to me: studying the Bible and the revolutionary Christian movement has led me to an understanding of historic materialism (¡*Yo creo en la justicia!*, p. 76).

In my own case it was daily life—in the light of faith—daily, growing contact with the poor and the oppressed—out of the demands of charity—that led me to an understanding of the Marxist dialectic and to a total political metanoia.

The "Murcian" families, the outlying districts, the workers, in Sabadell and Barcelona; the camp at Alto Aragón; the working families, the unemployed, the migrant field workers, the housemaids, the drifters of Sabadell, Barcelona, and Madrid; the colonized blacks of Guinea and Nigeria; the people of the *favelas,* the *"operarios,"* the segregated blacks, the northeasterners, the men in hiding, and all those who have been imprisoned, tortured and have died, for political reasons, in Brazil; the transient families, the *posseiros,* the peons, the Indians and the prostitutes of this Mato Grosso, of this Amazonia.... All these have been and are my judges, my teachers, and my prophets in revolution. To them I owe this unwieldy translation of the gospel of Jesus that I am now trying to live.

To them I owe it, them and so many martyrs—Christians, whether they knew it or not—whom I have known or read about, who gave their lives for the cause of the poor of the earth, for the cause of the new man. To one of them, Che Guevara, I dedicated a poem in my "Clamor Elemental." This poem has merited the scandal of the "good" and a pamphlet by the Repression. The poem came to me in the following way:

At night, until eleven, the city sleeping and an immense moon awakening, Manuel and I listened alone on the transistor, to the finals of the First University Festival of Popular Brazilian Music: "¡Que bacana!," "Senhora de luar," and then, "Ven companheiro,

Che!"—Come, comrade Che! a homage and cry for the
martyr of the continent.

Once again, Che Guevara. And America. And death.
And the poor. With a great peace, because I know that
in Christ everything is grace, and I hope in him
throughout all circumstances, however futile, sorrowful,
or paradoxical they may be.

I pray for Che. I feel that he, now, will have come to
know something of the supreme power of love's violence. "Without ever losing tenderness," he had
asked. . . .

The Araguaia, pierced by moonlight, beats at our feet,
like an artery. I feel the nearness of many particular
friends. I feel Latin America. I peacefully recall some
words by Loew, from the morning's meditation: In the
apostolate, it is necessary to know how to hope. All those
things in the gospel parables about the slowness of the
seed's growth. And here am I, not much of anything,
helping the gospel—and its revolution—to bear fruit in
this America of Che's which must become the America
of Christ. . . .

Some day I'll write a poem to my friend, Guevara.
¡God keep him in his peace! (*Diary:* October 1, 1968).

And one day I did write the poem.

CHE GUEVARA

And, at last, your death, too, called me
from out the dry light of Villagrande.
I, Che, go on believing
in love's violence: you yourself once said
that "we must steel ourselves
without ever losing tenderness."

But you called me. Even you.
(The sad themes we shared.
The many dying glances.
The maddening inertia of compassion.
The sage solutions given at a distance. . . .
America! The poor. That third world,
when there's only one world,
God's and men's!)

I hear our rebel youth, on the transistor,
singing of you,
while the Araguaia, like a living artery, beats at my feet,
pierced by the near-full moon.
All lights go out. And it is only night.
My far-off, future friends close in on me.
(Another song is wailing: "At least your
absence is real enough." . . . O the Presence
in whom I believe, Che,
for whom I live,
in whom I hope so passionately!
. . . But you must know enough, by now,
of answers and encounters.)

Rest in peace. And wait, secure,
your lungs cured
of the asthma of weariness;
your dying glance wiped clean of hate;
with no more arms, friend,
than the naked blade of your death.
(Dying is always winning
ever since that day when
Someone died for all, like all,
killed, like many. . . .)

Neither "the good"—on one side—
nor "the bad"—on the other—
will understand my song.
They'll say I'm just a poet.
They'll think that fashion has possessed me.
They'll note that I'm a "new-style" priest.
It's all the same to me!
We're friends
and I am talking with you now
across the death that joins us;
and I'm reaching you a branch of hope,
a whole flowering forest of
Latin American perennial jacarandas,
dear Che Guevara!

Péguy sought a "temporal revolution" for the eternal salvation of humanity. Camus complained because so many Christians had "decided to give up on generosity, so as to practice charity." The Brazilian humorist, Millor Fernandes, says that "what we call a political interview is really the act of talking about something we should be doing." All three remarks have much to commend them. And, speaking of the cause of the new man, I would like to propose that we be aware of them in life.

Come what may, this is what I believe: I truly believe in the cause of the new man.

I believe in another humanity, a more fraternal one, one which—in political parlance—I would call "socialized." The world needs to breathe the air of human harmony. All men must come to recognize each other as men, as brothers in the utopia of faith. I believe in the impossible and necessary new man!

I do not believe in racial or classist segregation. (Because there is but one image of God in man.)
I do not believe in slavery of any kind. (Because all of us have the right and duty to live in the freedom of sons in which Christ freed us.)
I do not believe in capitalism of any kind. (Because the real capital of man is man.)
I do not believe in the development of minorities or in the "developmentalist" development of the majority. (Because this "development" is not the new name for peace.)
I do not believe in progress at any cost. (Because man has been bought at the cost of Christ's blood.)
I do not believe in the mechanizing technology of those "who pray to the computer: our father art thou." (Because only the living God is our Father.)
I do not believe in the "consumer society." (Because only those are blessed who hunger and thirst after justice.)
I do not believe in the so-called order of the status quo. (Because the kingdom of God and men is a new heaven and a new earth.)
I do not believe in the heavenly city at the cost of the earthly city. (Because "the earth is the only road which can lead us to heaven.")
I do not believe in the earthly city at the cost of the heavenly city. (Because "we have here no lasting city, but seek the city that is to come.")
I do not believe in the old man. (Because I believe in the new man.)
I believe in the new man who is Jesus Christ Risen, the firstborn of every new man! Amen, Alleluia!

V

Total Hope

I have spoken about hope throughout this book, because hope has been my credo throughout the most conscious part of my life.

I am now going to concentrate on one aspect of the credo of hope that I have lived, and which I have come to affirm as my "sure and solid anchor" (Hb 6:19).

Because of my psychological makeup and the contingencies of my life, anxiety has followed me, like a shadow. Loneliness, too. And, many times, fear. And a wearing sense of responsibility. And also, a radical dissatisfaction.

I will transcribe four fragments from my diary that will bear this out:

I feel like disappearing, like not being anywhere, like not having to answer to anyone about anything (October 2, 1969).

Time, when it is not a concrete occasion for doing something, is a dangerous occasion for remembering, fearing, and desiring. To kill time with dignity is, sometimes, a difficult virtue (March 25, 1970).

The valiant are the ones who can overcome the much or little fear they have. The believers are those who overcome, in hope, all the doubts, the terrors and the bitternesses that necessarily invade us here, in this pilgrim land (February 25, 1970).

"The antidote for anxiety is choice," says the almanac of *Vozes*. But the work of choosing is never done: we go on doing it hour by hour, minute by minute. It is fidelity, what our elders used to call "perfection," the "Yes, Father," of Jesus (March 23, 1970).

"Prayer is hope's breathing. When we stop praying, we stop hoping," I also wrote. I don't hope, then, out of some natural, psychosomatic bent. I hope out of hope.

I saw death when I was two years old. They tell me that I was two years old, when the first image I remember was engraved on my memory. It was the little girl next door, with whom I used to play in the sand, by the sidewalk. Someone (I'm not sure who) took my little hand in their big hand, and led me to the room where, to the horror of my infant eyes, she died, beneath that rose-colored counterpane, beneath the silent glances of the grownups. . . .

Since then, I have seen many deaths. I have attended many dying people. I have meditated a great deal on death, almost to the point of the macabre. And I have died a number of times in anticipation.

I have come (masochism? education? the radical Spanish mystique?) to feel very close to death. . . , to feel that one day I would have to live again; so that I should not be tied down to this transitory life; so as to confirm the monotonous, incontrovertible, universal argument that, truly, "the figure of this world passes."

And for me, even now, death—every death—continues being the most serious thing in life. Just as the present life continues being the next most serious thing to the eternity to come.

I don't need anyone to remind me of human "nothingness" or of the futility of life. I recognizé myself all too clearly in the *coplas* of Jorge Manrique, in ascetical sermons, and in the acid pages of Qoheleth.

I can say—with gratitude, now—that death has come to cast a permanent shadow on the life that lies ahead. To live in dialogue with death does not cease to be a grace... when one believes.

The thing that I have always found most overwhelming about death is its being the condition of our "entry into eternity," of that great leap into the void. The next most overwhelming thing about death, is that it marks our life as a unique human adventure: every man dies alone.

Am I afraid to die? I know that I have not escaped death; no one can. Yet I have said that I have been asking for it—as a martyrdom—perhaps to tease it more gloriously as the torero teases the bull. Because a "killing" seems less fatal than a "wasting away," and—because one welcomes or provokes it—it seems more like a supreme and sporting act of life. (Or maybe it's my charism. There are charisms for living; why not charisms for dying?)

In any case, no matter how this strikes you, remember that I'm confessing *my* faith, with all its idiosyncrasies.

Some time ago, in Spain, I wrote my *Profecía extrema* (Last Prophecy). Years later I ratified, corrected, and enlarged it. It is now much closer to life, here, in this conflict-ridden Mato Grosso, where death by killing is not so extraordinary. (Last night I went to attend to a military policeman who had received a very serious gunshot wound. An aeronautics sergeant, accompanied by two hired killers, entered the hospital before me. Revolver in hand, he was asking questions about some new candidate to shoot. What a mixture: priest and gunmen, bullets and holy oils, nurses and patients, and the curious, in a hospital corridor....)

Last Prophecy: Ratified

I'll die standing, like the trees.
They'll kill me standing.

The sun, as chief witness, will set its seal
upon my twice-anointed body.

And the rivers and the sea
will make a roadway
of all my desires,
while the beloved forest will shake its treetops with
    rejoicing.

I will say to my words:
—I wasn't lying when I shouted you.
God will say to my friends:
—I certify
that he lived with you, hoping for this day.

In a flash, with death,
my life will come true.
At last, I will have loved!

One of the repellent, purifying tests of my hope, during these past few years, has been to witness so many daily, "stupid" deaths. The same is true of the constant news or sight of so many disasters and violent deaths brought about by the defiant conceit of technology and progress. The same is true again of all the voiceless suffering of innumerable children, born to suffer and to die, and of all the human misery that I am powerless to help. Finally, there is the persistent, growing, and insoluble problem of injustice, which is eating up the world and gnawing daily, here, at the very bones of Peace.

In the opening note to my *Clamor Elemental,* I wrote that "bitterness or sadness do not negate hope: they purify it (and commit it, I added later) and give it its earthly reason for being; they multiply it by dividing it. . . ."

Again I repeat it. And I add this confession-barb that Fr. Llanos sent me in a letter: "We have hope, but they are the ones that are waiting in hope." [*Tr. note: There is a special ambiguity in the verb "esperar." It can mean "to hope," or simply "to wait."*] My faith, for a long time now, is hope.

And, as Cardinal Feltin remarked: "Christian hope is not just an 'afterwards' that helps us live; it is not something; it is Some-one."

My hope has a first and last name: JESUS-CHRIST/ RISEN.

The Passover of Jesus Christ, who is "our Passover," is the real reason for my hope. I hope because he is risen and is "the resurrection and the life."

When, as a seminarian, I discovered that grace is somehow "already" glory ("groping glory," we used to call it), and that here on earth we were living that same, unique, eternal life we would be living in eternity, then all the foundations for my dichotomies between this life and the next crumbled at a single blow. (I'm not saying that the "how" of that eternal life here, is not profoundly different from what it is there. Anyone knows that earth is "not yet" heaven!)

Then all of human history was really the unique history of salvation. Every attempted human joy and every human failure; every achievement, every step of man; the history-bound hope of the Marxist struggle; above all, the deaths of those who gave their lives for the cause of man; the strokes of those who—perhaps blindly—strove to build a better future—all of these were being transformed into an eschatological tension, into a "profession—cogent or crazy—of total hope." And "hope never fails" (Rom 5:5).

"Earth is the only road that can lead us to heaven," I have repeated endlessly, in the words of the unforgettable Père Charles of our missionary readings.

Every waiting became hope. "Knowing how to wait in hope" was knowing how to live actively and alert, with our lamps filled and burning.... "If only we are fearless and keep our hope high" (Hb 3:6).

No, Camus, hope is not resignation. Resignation is only hope's silence. But hope has words of eternal life! To resign oneself is not to hope. It may even be the very opposite (*Diary*, April 1, 1970).

According to Ligier, Paul discovered sin as a universal reality that resists the gospel. Paul also discovered, as he himself says, that where sin abounded, grace did more abound.

Hope "deciphers" everything "into hope." Hope is like Moema, the Indian girl in the story, "reflected in her face, even death was beautiful." Through hope, nature, with all its mysteries and terrors, becomes the harmonious cosmos. Through hope, "society" becomes humanity, humanity becomes church; history becomes kingdom and Parousia.

For me, Teilhard was no visionary.

I do not "understand" the world. I am surprised every day by man. I even find myself to be one big, daily, surprise. I do not understand life. I understand death even less. (One of our volunteer gravediggers, who was burying a peasant friend of his, remarked: "What we're planting here, only God knows how to make grow.") But I believe. I hope! (Don't ask me any questions about hell—which I neither deny nor understand. I know that it is a doₓma of faith which cannot contradict that universal love, which is God, or the mystery of Christ, which is the redemption of man and the world, or the mystery of man, created out of love, born into who knows what sin, but reborn in the grace of Christ.)

What they call the dialogue between the church and the world, is much more than dialogue. The church and the world are not two realities lined up face to face, or even in parallel. Where and when does the world begin, that the church does not begin?

"God so loved the world that he gave his only Son" (Jn 3:16). It was in the world that the Word was made flesh, and it is the sacramental mission of the church to discover and proclaim and realize the Word as incarnate in the world.

Secularization and the new sacralization, the theology of transcendence and the theology of liberation form only one perspective and have but one task. Where does nature end and grace begin? "Everything is grace!" Everything is Christ: his glory and his cross, the thirst for him, the face of him in whom we believe we see God, or the anonymous face of anyone of the "least of my brethren" whom one feeds or clothes or enlightens or defends. . . .

I believe that God is love.
I believe that the creator does not mock his creatures.
I believe that Christ has conquered sin and death.
I believe that death in Christ is already resurrection.
I believe that "the whole creation has been groaning in

labor, in hopes of being freed from the servitude of corruption, so as to share in the glorious freedom of the sons of God" (Cf. Rom 8:20-22).

I believe that on that day, God himself "will wipe away every tear from our eyes, and death shall be no more, neither shall there be mourning nor crying nor pain any more, for the former things have passed away" (Rev 21:4).

I believe that when what we shall be has been disclosed, "we shall be like him, for we shall see him as he is" (1 Jn 3:2) "face to face" (1 Cor 13:12).

"When we arrive, we will be fully men," said Ignatius Martyr. "Free, free at last!" sighed Martin Luther King.

Meanwhile, with all those who believe, with all those who struggle, with John and with the spouse, I cry out the most certain word that has ever been written, in this kingdom of death and hope: "Come, Lord Jesus!"

Are we all going to work together for his coming?